Multiple Streams of Determination

VOLUME 1

➤ A New Chapter ⬅

Wimbrey Training Systems

MULTIPLE STREAMS OF DETERMINATION
A New Chapter

© 2011 Wimbrey Training Systems

All rights reserved. No part of this publication may be reproduced, stored in any retrieval system, or transmitted in any form or by any means, mechanical, photocopying, recording, or otherwise, without permission in writing from the publisher, except by a reviewer, who may quote brief passages in a review.

For information, please contact:

Wimbrey Training Systems
8708 Woodfell Court
Dallas, TX 75249

www.JohnnyWimbrey.com

info@JohnnyWimbrey.com

ISBN-13: 978-0-9835003-0-8

1 2 3 4 5 6 7 8 9 10

Table of Contents

1	**Mastering the Mind**	
	Johnny Wimbrey	*1*
2	**Who Needs a Runway?**	
	Vernice Armour	*13*
3	**Creating the Fire Within**	
	Matt Morris	*23*
4	**Poetry of Love**	
	Terri Scarborough	*29*
5	**Defining Moments**	
	Marc Accetta	*37*
6	**Why Ask "Why"?**	
	Yvette Shaw	*47*
7	**Don't Sleep Through Your Wake Up Call**	
	Terry Ellison	*57*
8	**Separated To Be Elevated**	
	John Di Lemme	*65*
9	**Blueprint of a Dream**	
	Bobby Minor	*71*

10	**Determination For Freedom**
	Nakis Theocharides 79

11	**Don't Believe the Hype!**
	Terry McGee 87

12	**Changing to a New You So the "Real" You Can Shine Through**
	Les Brown 95

13	**Choose to Win Now**
	David Imonitie, Jr. 103

14	**I Am In Love With My Life**
	Georgina Druce 113

15	**Unlimited Power**
	Sean Conner 127

16	**From Corporation to Liberation**
	George Adamides 135

17	**Defining Moments**
	Jim Rohn 145

A Message from the Publisher

I've personally spent $10,000 to attend a four-day seminar and had my life changed by just one thing I heard. I'm not saying the other information wasn't good; it was just that that one moment changed me forever. You see, we never know beforehand when we may have a moment. It could be something we see, something we hear, or something we read. That one "nugget" might be all we need to experience a breakthrough.

Because of that, we have brought together some of the most inspiring men and women from across the globe. From London to the Bahamas by way of Long Island, New York; Atlanta, Georgia; Miami, Florida; Fort Worth, Texas; and many points in-between, these stories will surely take you to places you have never been before. With stories of overcoming adversity, keys to a healthy marriage, bringing your dreams to life, making a difference in the world, becoming a self-made millionaire by the age of twenty, and several others, you may very well have a "moment" when you read this book.

Typically, great things have to happen to bring together these kinds of people in a single place. Some might say that the stars and moon must first align to make it happen. Whatever the case may be, this book is filled with information, insight, and wisdom from great people who have done

Multiple Streams of Determination

great things. The beauty of this book is that they want to give something to you, not take something from you. It has been said that knowledge is power and that's true to a certain extent. But true power comes from applied knowledge, or impartation. Make sure you apply what you learn.

It is my prayer that each and every one of you who read this book will not be afraid to use it as it is intended, to take you to a higher level. Don't be afraid to mark it up, make notes, and highlight the words or phrases that really speak to you. Use this book to inspire yourself to greatness!

I would like to say thank you to all of the men and women who shared their stories in this wonderful piece of work and I would like to give a very special thanks to Les Brown for sharing his insight and wisdom.

—Johnny D. Wimbrey
President, Wimbrey Training Systems

Foreword

I am normally asked to write the foreword for a book that I'm not a part of in terms of being the author. In this case I have the double honor of not only writing the foreword but also being a featured author in a book that is the first in a series of life changing books. Self-investment, which is investing in one's self, is the greatest investment a person could ever make.

It has been said that the richest plots of land in the world aren't the diamond mines in South Africa, nor the oil fields in the Middle East, but rather the graveyards and cemeteries because that's where people and their dreams are buried. There are life-changing and world-changing people and ideas which will never be heard because they never had the chance to reach the masses.

Using their life experiences, these authors have proven that if you have a willingness to do whatever is required, and take the initiative to pursue your dreams, you can make some incredible things happen.

If you are willing to elevate your life beyond your circumstances and allow that to become your life mission, coupled with a strong belief in yourself and in a power greater than yourself, the possibilities of reinventing your life and transforming who you are now into who you can become are unlimited.

This book is designed to empower you with the secret process of success used by those who not only talk the talk, but also more importantly, walk the walk.

You will go through step-by-step proven methods to transform your life and experience the health, wealth, and happiness we all want. I found every chapter inspiring and enlightening, as I'm sure you will.

Multiple Streams of Determination

These people have accomplished many tremendous things in their lives, and they are sharing the things that they have learned along the way with you. Read it with an open mind and an open heart.

There have been three volumes of Multiple Streams of Inspiration that have changed lives. This is the first volume of Multiple Streams of Determination, a New Chapter, and like its "cousins" before it this book will change your life as well; I guarantee it.

Les Brown

Chapter 1

The Psychology of Winning

JOHNNY WIMBREY

Winning isn't everything, but wanting to win is.
~ VINCE LOMBARDI

Success leaves clues. There are no coincidences to winning. No one wins by chance or luck. Winners win because they want to win. Winners think about winning all the time. Best-selling recording artist Nelly released an inter- national hit entitled "What Does It Take to Be Number One?" The chorus line says number "two is not a winner and three nobody remembers." This album went straight to the top of the charts and made Nelly an international phenomenon. He wrote the song before he became number one in the public's eyes, yet he understood the concept of winning and attitude. Winners eat, sleep, and

Multiple Streams of Determination

breathe the concept of victory—of being number one. If you want to be in first place, you first must see yourself there. You must sell yourself on the fact that you are a winner and that you are number one, long before it's obvious to others. "Faith is the substance of things hoped for and the evidence of things not seen." You must think like a winner in order to become one.

Terry L. Hornbuckle authored a book titled See Your Future, Be Your Future. In this book he talks about how important—and how necessary it is—for you to see your future in order for your hopes, aspirations, and goals to become a manifested reality. You must believe without a shadow of a doubt that you deserve to win. And you must practice seeing yourself as the winner in order to be a winner.

> *Only a man who knows what it is like to be defeated can reach down to the bottom of his soul and come up with an extra ounce of power it takes to win when the match is even.*
> ~ MUHAMMAD ALI

Voted USA Today's Athlete of the Century, heavyweight champion Muhammad Ali mastered the psychology of winning. Long before Ali was the greatest fighter of all time, he told the world he was the greatest. Long before the world knew who he was, he told the local gyms that he was the greatest. And long before he became confident enough to become outspoken, he told himself he was the greatest. Ali first convinced himself that he was the greatest before he could convince anyone else. What's more important to remember than any of the above is this: Not only is it necessary for you to continually remind yourself that you are a winner, it is mandatory for your opponent to see, hear, and feel your confidence in your own abilities to win. When your opponent begins to imagine you winning, half of the battle is already won.

The Psychology of Winning

Other people's opinion of you does not have to become your reality.

~ LES BROWN

Who is your opponent? Like your foe, your opponent can be anything or anyone who tries to keep you from coming out of the box. My opponents are the odds that stand against me. Society and statistics tell us that because I'm biracial, was born in the projects, lived on welfare, had an alcoholic for a father, and came from a single-parent home that I supposedly will never have any control of what ultimately will determine my future. According to society, I was supposed to have suffered emotionally at the hands of my peers because of my undetermined race; I am supposed to be struggling with alcoholic tendencies; I'm supposed to be socially and economically depressed; and my ever experiencing a successful marriage is not likely to happen. But my reality is very different. I could have had problems in school about my race, but it was obvious that I was confident and very satisfied with who I was. In high school I ended up being Homecoming King, Most Likely to Be Remembered, and Class Favorite. I don't have any dependency on alcohol, I live a very nice lifestyle, and my wife and I have been married happily for over five years and are still best friends today.

Listen very closely. Never let others' experiences become your reality! You are the only one who can officially deter- mine who and what you will become. If you see yourself in society's box, that's where you will be. Never let anyone create your world for you, because they will always create it too small.

Am I a freak of nature? No! I am simply programmed by God to be the head and not the tail; to be above and not beneath anyone or anything. I was designed to win, and so I choose to walk with my footsteps toward my God-given right. I am mentally programmed to win. I am a record breaker! I am confident and not arrogant.

Multiple Streams of Determination

Everyone experiences hard times and struggles, but all winners have one thing in common, and that is that we don't like to lose. Society has programmed us to think that if you're having trouble in your marriage, get a divorce. Almost all situations have an easy way out, but the prize for the race is not always given to the quick; instead, it is given to the one who perseveres and finishes the race. Winners understand that through the thick and thin, we must win! Failure is not an option for winners. They say winners never quit. I can guarantee you a quitter will never be a winner!

A true winner also understands the importance of surrounding himself or herself with other winners. I have made it a personal goal in my life to constantly introduce myself to—and continuously surround myself with—people who stretch me. All winners understand that you must get out of your comfort zone. You can't learn how to swim in shallow waters. Don't be afraid of the deep. It's hard to move to a higher level if everyone around you is beneath you or on the same level as you. I don't mean beneath you as in you are better as a person than they are, because we know that we are ALL created equally. What I mean is, for example, if you want to become an executive at your job, then you need to expose yourself to the mentality of an executive. There are a lot of people who are, or have been, where you are trying to go. You cannot follow a parked car. Hang around winners and you will become a winner too!

The Importance of Having Mentors

Winners understand and value the importance of having mentors. I have found that in many cases people use the word "mentor" very loosely. A mentor, first of all, is some- one that you know personally. You may admire someone on TV, but he or she is not your mentor unless you have access to him or her. You choose your mentor; your mentor does not choose you. You may be approached by someone who wants to put you under his or her wing and guide you, but until you choose to go, he or she is not your men- tor. In addition, your mentor must accept the role, or he or she is not a mentor. A mentor should be able to correct you on the spot; you submit immediately and take heed of his or her direction. This is why you choose your men- tor. Because the moment you begin to unwillingly receive advice, correction, or even open rebuke, then he or she is no longer your mentor.

Synonyms for the word mentor: Teacher, Adviser, Tutor, Counselor, Guru, Guide. Webster's dictionary defines the mentor as "A trusted counselor or guide."

In order to have a mentor, you must be a protégé! Synonyms and definition of the word protégé: dependent, student, disciple, one who accepts the charge. You can have different mentors for different areas of your life. For example, you may have a physical mentor, a spiritual mentor, and a financial mentor. It's great if all of these are the same person, but it's not necessary.

How Do You Choose a Mentor?

1. He/she has something that you would also like to have or experience. Example: You play the saxophone and he/she is very good with the sax.

2. He/she agrees to mentor you.

3. He/she must be someone who can tell you NO!

4. He/she has a lifestyle you respect in every facet.

5. He/she must be someone that you can be honest with, no matter what!

Multiple Streams of Determination

> *In the multitude of counselors there is safety.*
> ~KING SOLOMON

Mentors' jobs are to protect us. That's why it's very important that we be open and honest with them so they can tell, show, and give us everything we need that is in our best interests. True mentors will tell us what we need to hear, instead of what we want to hear. Great mentors will inspect what they expect. In other words, they won't just tell us what to do; they will follow up or make sure we report our results. Mentors are not dictators but advisors who want us to succeed without sacrificing our integrity. Great mentors will never ask us to compromise good character to get to the top.

A great financial mentor will show you how to master your money, instead of your money mastering you. When your money tells you what to do, you are in trouble, but when you can tell your money what to do, you can and will experience true wealth.

I once read that open rebuke is better than hidden love. A great mentor understands that he or she must tell it to you like it is.

A great winner is also a great protégé who will apply the advice from the mentor that he or she chose. A mentor has every right to terminate a relationship with a rebellious protégé. Likewise, the protégé has every right to terminate a relationship with his or her mentor. Keep in mind, if you find yourself jumping from mentor to mentor because they are not what you expected them to be, chances are they are not the ones with the problems.

I will tell you from experience that there are plenty of times I have gotten my feelings hurt by my mentors, but remember, I chose them. Winners are not afraid of constructive criticism and understand that it takes iron to sharpen iron.

The Psychology of Winning

My wife Crystal and I are very blessed to have incredible marital mentors, Eben and Sara Conner, who hold us accountable to each other. We chose them; they did not choose us. They have counseled us on several occasions. I must admit that when I know I am right, I am very quick to call them to referee when Crystal and I are having intense fellowships (arguments). I do confess that the majority of the times I call them in so Crystal can get help (because I am right). Usually, I end up being the one getting the most help.

Did you know that it is possible to deceive yourself? Deception would not be deception if it were obvious! You can be off track and not know it. And without correct navigation you will eventually crash.

Crystal and I know that Eben and Sara want us to win in every facet of our lives. And since they have our best interests at heart, we agree to submit to their wisdom. Wisdom is the application of knowledge. So when they share their knowledge, as their protégés we must apply their instructions, regardless of who is at fault. A winner knows when to swallow his or her pride in order to resolve a higher cause and/or purpose. Winners understand that it is impossible to win by themselves.

Winners MUST Win!

Winners don't see success as an option; we see it as something that we must have. Average people want to win, but winners must win. While the majority of the world is talking about what they want to happen, the mentality of the winner is focused on what must happen. As a winner, you must be able to convert every one of your wants to your musts. When you want something, it's optional. But when you must have something, it's non-negotiable. Everyone wants to be successful; only a very few must be successful.

So how do you turn your wants into your musts? I've done seminars across the nation on this topic. And when I ask the audience to give me a list of things that are a must in their lives, here are some of the common answers that I get.

Things People Must Have Or Do

- be at work on time
- pay bills on time
- eat
- bathe
- buy groceries
- pay taxes

Here is a common list of answers that I get when I ask for things they want.

Things People Want To Have Or Do

- eat healthy
- exercise
- go on vacation
- pray every day
- give to charity
- spend more time with the family

OK, by now you should get the point. The only difference between the things that you must have or do and the things that you want to have or do is you. Your attitude determines your ability to succeed.

Typically, the things that most people see as a must are tied to negative consequences. For example, if you don't eat, you starve. Or if you don't show up for work on time, you will get fired. In other words, most people are programmed to perform in order to prevent immediate negative reactions. You have a why for all your musts.

On the other hand, there are the few who are driven by the thrill of success. These individuals understand that they must do today what others don't, to have tomorrow what others won't. These are the ones who have the ability to make things happen, and who are self-disciplined. It is very important to have a reason, or a why, for everything that you want.

Example

I "must" be successful because I "want" to leave an inheritance for my children's children.

When you find your why in everything that you want and become passionate with a burning desire for the end result, your wants will become musts. Therefore, you must find your why for all of your wants.

Wants + Whys = Musts

- I MUST eat healthy to live longer.
- I MUST exercise for energy and for good health.
- I MUST go on vacation because I work hard.
- I MUST pray every day to stay spiritually strong.
- I MUST give to charity to save lives.
- I MUST spend more time with my family to show my love.

My cause is bigger than me, and because my wants have whys that are much more important than selfish desires, I am willing to fight for the end result. You must be willing to fight for the cause of your wants. It's hard to fight for something without a cause, so connect all of your wants to all of your whys so that all of your dreams will come to fruition.

About the Author

Internationally-acclaimed talk show host, author, and motivational-speaking giant Johnny Wimbrey lives by one rule: Don't let your past determine your future. Living a real- life "G to Gent" story, Wimbrey continues to inspire and change the lives of corporate execs and inner city kids alike.

After enduring a challenging road and some dispiriting experiences, Johnny managed to dramatically turn his life around and has become one of the most inspirational speakers of our time. Growing up in Fort Worth, Texas, and dealing with the split of his parents at a young age, Johnny learned early on that the only person one can truly rely on is oneself. Forced to fend for himself, he looked to the streets and began an involvement with drugs and gangs. The murder of a close friend served as an eye-opener to Johnny and made him decide that it was finally time to "flip the switch".

With a fresh new outlook and his mind set on success, Johnny set out to reinvent himself, only to learn that significant change did not come easy. Having come from a past with more hardship than opportunity, he found that finding a new career would be a challenge. However, Johnny's determination to succeed surmounted the struggle, and he soon landed a successful career in insurance and credits. His new career gave him a stability that he had never experienced, and more importantly, was a product of his own hard work and genius.

Johnny continued to excel in the insurance business and began spreading his knowledge to new recruits. It was during this time that he realized that he had a remarkable capacity to speak. After much pursuit he began launching his seminars in 2000, which focus on discovering the psychology of success and the traits of a winning mind-set. Since then, Johnny's goal has been to inspire others with the success secrets that his own life has proven to work. In the last year, Johnny has spread his life-enhancing words to audiences around the world, speaking in London, Australia, Singapore, South Africa, Amsterdam, Israel, The Virgin Islands—a list that continues to grow. Johnny has travelled over 170 thousand miles internationally to speak!

In addition to speaking Johnny has written the best-selling book, "From the Hood to Doing Good", an inspirational work that motivates people to put past pains behind them. Johnny's work has inspired people with a wide variety of struggles to make the positive decisions that have led them to significant life changes. In addition to his book, Johnny has co-authored "Multiple Streams of Inspiration" and "Conversations on Success", both of which inspire greatness. Johnny also anchors a powerful DVD collection called "Think and Win Big", which offers mental strategies and gives profound insight into the kind of wisdom needed for success. Johnny recently launched a new magazine entitled "Success University", which highlights inspirational stories to motivate people.

When not out spreading world-shaking words of wisdom, Johnny is a loving father who enjoys spending time with his family, riding his Harley, and like any true Texan, watching football.

For more information please visit www.johnnywimbrey.com.

Chapter 2

Who Needs a Runway?

VERNICE ARMOUR

Would you like to know the success strategies of an attack helicopter pilot? Would like to know the formula for putting your life's goals on the right track?

I was providing protection for Marines as they headed north to Baghdad. The strong smell of gunpowder seeping into the cockpit stung my nostrils as we destroyed the enemy's vehicles and equipment below. Suddenly, I spotted a gray mist cloud in the atmosphere about fifty to one hundred yards away.

"Did you see that?" I asked Ruvalcaba, my fellow pilot.

At first, neither one of us knew what had created the cloud. Then we realized it was caused by air bursts from rocket-propelled grenades (RPGs). Fortunately, it didn't hit us. Then we saw another one, then

Multiple Streams of Determination

several, and they were getting closer. As the Lead Cobra pulled off from another attack, his aircraft received a crippling shot. He had to

head back...NOW! In a matter-of-fact tone, I heard him tell us he had been hit and needed to return to the forward operating base. My heart was pounding and I prepared myself to now be in the lead aircraft of this battle.

I didn't know the extent of the damage, and even though it was only six miles away, I didn't know whether they'd make it back to the base. I remember looking at them as they turned westward and watched as they departed the area. I prayed for them to make it back to safety. I tried not to visualize what could happen to them if they didn't make it. I couldn't give the hit cobra any more attention or energy. My aircraft had just become the lead for the remaining assaults. I quickly turned my head back to the front of the aircraft and started scanning for the enemy and getting ready for the next attack.

Ruvalcaba, the section leader, immediately turned our section back into the ambush. The battle raged on, but finally, we had deployed all our weapons and the troops on the ground were able to push back the enemy. Before we headed back to base the troops were making their way forward again towards Baghdad.

As we headed back to base, I finally realized how quickly I was breathing and took a deep breath. When we made it back, I saw the helicopters that left the fight earlier sitting on the deck and I was able to let out a deep sigh of relief. We had all made it back safely. It was time to cherish the moment of being alive and preparing to go out on the next mission.

Who Needs a Runway?

How did I end up being this pilot who was flying over the deserts of Iraq protecting the men and women on the ground? It all started with a desire. Ever since the age of 4, believe it or not, I wanted to be a cop that rode a horse downtown! When I was 6 I got my very first pony. I just knew I was half way to my goal! I was able to go to college through the use of student loans and grants, which didn't leave any money to hang out with.

As I was walking down the hall in the student union, I saw a flyer on the wall that said "Free Trip to Mardi Gras"! As I got closer and could read the fine print, it stated all you had to do was join the women's ROTC rifle team. After thinking about it for less than 30 seconds, I headed over to the building and signed up! I trained for a few months with the team and then we headed down to New Orleans. I had the most amazing time. In fact, I was so inspired that I decided to enlist in the Army Reserves. So, I took the spring semester off from my sophomore year and went through Basic Training in Ft. Jackson, SC.

Why did I join the Army? Because I had found something that would help me **prepare for my passion**! We might not be where we want to be right now, but what can we do to help us get there? At 19, I wasn't old enough to go through police academy (you had to be 21) but I WAS old enough to join the service. There, I could learn about physical fitness, esprit de corps, disciple, uniformity…everything I thought that would help me get accepted to police academy and maybe even save my butt once I got out on the streets.

When I graduated from training, I headed back to school and made up all my classes during the summer session. That next fall, I joined Army ROTC, the actual program because I wanted to continue to gain an advantage…a strategic advantage. When you enroll in the ROTC

Multiple Streams of Determination

program, one of the requirements is attending leadership training for six weeks during the summer. What I saw during that summer would change my life.

It was career day and I wanted to do anything that would give me experience shooting a gun (or blowing something up)! I was with my battle buddy and she already knew she was going to be a pilot. I wanted nothing to do with flying. After half the day goes by with me dragging her around to almost every display there is, she asks if we can finally go over to the aviation tent. I took a deep breath of resignation and followed her across the huge field to where the aviation tent was tucked away in the edge of the trees.

I moved the flap back and walked into the dimly lit tent. As my eyes adjusted I looked toward to the back of the tent and saw a black woman in a flight suit! I couldn't believe what I was seeing! I said to myself, "Man…why didn't I think of that!?" I spoke to her for several minutes, then we headed back to finish up our day, but a very strong seed had just been planted.

Let me say right here it's all about access and exposure! What are you giving yourself access to? What are you exposing yourself to? In my case it was a complete different future than I had envisioned. Although I was extremely interested in pursuing aviation, I ended up receiving an invitation in the mail that asked me to finish taking the tests to get onto the Nashville Police Department. I accepted faster than humanly possible and found myself graduating from police academy in December of 1996.

Who Needs a Runway?

After a while on the force, I had passed the interview and testing to become a motorcycle officer. A year or so later, I found myself working as a police officer in Tempe Arizona. But, I couldn't forget that image of that woman in a flight suit. I decided I wanted to go for it and take the opportunity and challenge of becoming a pilot. I always had the opportunity to be a cop. There was a guy in my academy class that was older than everybody and we called him Pappy! So, off I went.

I joined the Marine Corps, went through Officer Candidates School, The Basic School, then off to flight school. The rest, as they say, is herstory. I ended up being the Marine Corps firs black female pilot and America's first African American female combat pilot. But it all started with a vision and that vision lead to a plan.

As a pilot, we were taught a very specific plan for carrying out our missions. I'd like to share a few of the most important steps with you below.

1. Create a Flight Plan
2. Pre-flight
3. Take-off, execute and fly the mission
4. Land
5. De-brief

Phase One: Create a plan. Do you have a flight plan? What is the plan you have for your life and your career? Where do you want to go? What do you want to do? When you are sitting on your front porch in the sunset of your life at age 70, 80 or beyond, what do you want to have accomplished? What do you want your legacy to have been? I'd like to give you a few exercises over the next few paragraphs.

Multiple Streams of Determination

Exercise 1: Take out pen and paper and spend a few moments writing down some of the top things that you would like to accomplish in your life. Give yourself a deadline. When are you going to start working on it? Remember, you don't have to know how you are going to accomplish this goal to start!

Phase Two: Conduct a thorough pre-flight. You need to inspect the aircraft you are getting ready to fly into the air. Is the plan you have created for your goals, dreams or career a plan you can stick with? Is it capable of getting you up in the air? Is it worthy of being flown? Only YOU know the answers to these questions. There will be many people who question what you want to do and your dreams in life. The secret is YOU have the faith and believe in what you are doing. Just ask Bill Gates or Tyler Perry, and if you don't know who these gentlemen are Google them and read their stories. They will absolutely inspire you!

Exercise Two: List some of the aspects of your plan that might need more clarity before commencing. Do you have the right qualifications or do you need to acquire them? Do you have everything you need for your flight already set-up in your "cockpit of life"? Do you need to go back to school for additional training? Look at your plan and write down 3-5 points that you have to support your plan.

Phase Three: Take off from where you are! This phase is my favorite! Who told you that you were a jet or plane and need a long runway? You have the choice to be an attack helicopter. The number one advantage of being a helicopter and not a plane is that you can take off from right

Who Needs a Runway?

where you are. You don't need a runway! How many people in your life do you know that are never ready to take action in their lives. It's seems they're always "getting ready or preparing to execute instead of just taking off! One of my favorite Les Brown quotes is, "You don't have to be great to get started, but you have to get started to be great!"

Exercise Three: Write down 3-5 things you think you need to do in order to take the next step. Notice I said take the next step, not complete your mission. You don't have to know how to complete the goal in order to get started. Just start!

Phase Four: Pick out your spot and land. What's your end goal and how do you need to maneuver in order to get down on the ground where you want to be. As you are pursuing your goals in life, always have a direction and idea of where you are going and what success looks like to YOU. Everyone's definition can be a little different. Make sure are following the desire in your heart.

Exercise Four: Write down your mission statement and definition of success.

Phase Five: Review, Recharge and Re-Attack! You're on the ground. You have completed your mission. Did it turn out the way you wanted it to or do you need to create another plan and go back out? In this phase you are going to review how you chose to tackle the mission of completing your goals, dreams or desires. Whether it was for life or business, the same basic process is utilized. Whether you need to go back out and work on that particular goal again or you are ready to make a new plan, you need to recharge and get your engines ready. Lastly, with your focus and intensity being laser sharp, you head back out to create the life and career you've always dreamed of!

Exercise Five: Write down you definition of success. What it means to you. What are the consequences if you don't accomplish your goal? What are the rewards if you do accomplish your goal?

Why is this particular goal so important to you?

Those of you familiar with my philosophy know I believe a breakthrough mentality creates a breakthrough life. For a free investigative report on the Five Secrets of the Successful that you MUST know and more tips on how to create that life for yourself visit my website at www.VerniceArmour.com.

"Do what average people do, have what average people have. I don't want to be average, do you?"   -Vernice Armour

About the Author

Vernice, aka *"FlyGirl"*, knows a little something about focus, commitment, and defying the odds. After accomplishing her dream of becoming a police officer, she decided, at age 24, to become an Officer in the Marine Corps and a combat pilot. Only 3 years later, she was the United States Marine Corps' first African American female pilot and, shortly after, was recognized as America's First African American Female Combat pilot by the Department of Defense.

Upon completion of two tours in Iraq and leaving the military, Vernice leveraged her experience and conceptualized the Zero to Breakthrough™ Success Model. After leaving the military, she launched VAI Consulting and Training, LLC. By applying

Who Needs a Runway?

the Zero to Breakthrough™ Success Model to her own company, Vernice produced over six-figures in revenue within the first 12 months! Her passion is helping others create similar results.

As featured on Oprah Winfrey, CNN, Tavis Smiley, NPR and others, Vernice Armour's dynamic style and presentation methods have inspired hundreds of organizations and individuals. Her blend of high-energy presentation with humorous anecdotes and commanding content educate and edify while it engages and entertains.

Vernice ultimately impacts organizations and individuals with an understanding of the passion and leadership required to excel. Through her keynotes, executive and group coaching, seminars and executive retreats, Vernice conveys messages of Zero to Breakthrough™ through her unique insight and life strategy: "Acknowledge the obstacles... Don't give them power!" Now, as a speaker, coach and consultant, her infectious energy, warmth and humor make each keynote speech as memorable as it is valuable.

Among her many accomplishments, Vernice has been awarded as a pioneering pilot, including her commanding role in technology and engineering. This amazing lady was also the first African American woman on the Nashville Police Department's motorcycle squad, Camp Pendleton's 2001 Female Athlete of the Year, two-time titleholder in Camp Pendleton's annual Strongest Warrior Competition, and a running back for the San Diego Sunfire women's professional football team. Vernice's first book, Zero to Breakthrough™" (Penguin) is due for release in the first quarter of 2011.

For more information on Vernice please visit: www.

Chapter 3

Creating the Fire Within

MATT MORRIS

After interviewing hundreds of wildly successful entrepreneurs, I've found one common thread that runs through them: The ability to harness a white heat of passion that spills out and gets all over the people around them. I'm sure you've been around people like that, people who just have a charisma that makes you feel good to be around them and leaves you feeling better about yourself after being in their presence.

That special charisma is what I call their *passion*. It's an intense emotion that drives them to succeed, a gut feeling that burns within them and fuels their inner being, their essence, to great achievement. It took me a while, but I learned the value of passion myself. Before I did, however, I had to experience extreme lows.

Multiple Streams of Determination

I can well remember the turning point in my life, the point at which I finally got it, when I finally made the mental shift and vowed that I would no longer accept mediocrity in my life. At that point I made the real commitment to creating the life of my dreams and living a life filled with passion. We're all motivated by either the avoidance of pain or the desire for pleasure. Unfortunately, what it took for me to have the lights turn on was an extreme amount of pain in my life. When I hit rock bottom, I finally woke up.

I started a business at twenty-one years old. Because of my lack of discipline and extreme lack of vision for my life, I was out of business within nine months. I found myself buried in approximately twenty thousand dollars in credit card debt. I was so broke, I couldn't afford to make the minimum payments on my credit cards or even pay rent.

After my failed entrepreneurial venture, I took a job as a pool salesman traveling in southern Louisiana in the sweltering heat of July and August. Because I didn't get paid commissions until the pool actually got installed, I ended up living out of my little red Honda Civic five to six nights a week, parking underneath shade trees so I wouldn't wake up being cooked by the sun.

Because I couldn't afford the luxury of staying in a motel with a shower, I bathed in gas station bathrooms. Late one night when I found myself in a city without an open gas station, I actually showered in the rain, standing underneath the runoff from the roof of a church.

I remember it as though it were yesterday. I got back in my car that night, laughing out loud at being the absolute definition of pathetic. I realized that I *had* to find a way to turn my life around.

That very night I popped in a cassette tape by a man who would soon become my mentor—Tony Robbins. Tony told his story of living out

Creating the Fire Within

of a four-hundred-square-foot apartment, which, given my circumstances, actually sounded pretty luxurious to me. He told of going from living an average existence to earning more than a million dollars a year in personal income. One of the things he had done at an early age was to read more than seven hundred books in the field of personal development. He also talked about modeling other people and noted that to be a success, you simply needed to figure out what that successful person did and do the same thing.

I put two and two together and decided that I would, like Tony, start reading everything I could get my hands on that would help me train and develop myself into a success. I started spending every spare moment in bookstores, pouring myself into books on sales, wealth generation, leadership, motivation, communication skills, and anything else that would propel me forward.

I read at least one book every two or three days and was particularly influenced by one of Tony's books. He stressed the importance of writing lists of everything you wanted in life and assigning deadlines for achieving those things. The simple exercise of putting dreams and goals on paper opened up a whole new world of passion. I literally saw and believed that I could live the life of my dreams. I quickly learned that dreams are the fuel that fires your passion.

I began visualizing myself having and living the life of my dreams. I saw a world in which everything I wanted was possible for me. I visualized earning millions of dollars, being able to take exotic vacations around the world, contributing millions of dollars to charity, helping other people become financially free, and being a leader that other leaders would follow. Now, just eight years later, I have come to the complete understanding that the more you visualize your dreams, the more you harness your passion. I've also come to

Multiple Streams of Determination

see that the more passion you live in your life, the more results you create.

I heard a saying many years ago that inspires me to this day and I suggest that you adopt it in your life as well if you desire to be a leader: "Get on fire for your passion and others will come from all over to watch you burn!"

It's that "getting on fire" that's allowed me to go from adversity to prosperity. It's my passion that's allowed me to be the top money earner in sales organizations with thousands of other salespeople, that's allowed me to travel all over the world, that's allowed me to help countless other people earn six-figure incomes, that's allowed me to generate millions of dollars and to be the CEO and founder of one of the largest personal development companies in the world, Success University.

Because of my passion for helping others achieve success, and our team's passion for making a difference in the world, we've been able to attract some of the greatest speakers, trainers, and authors in the entire personal development industry. We now generate millions of dollars in sales every year, but more important, we are helping people all over the world achieve financial and personal success in their lives. I now wake up every morning 100 percent committed to living every day of my life enjoying and giving to others God's gift of love, happiness, and passion. Not bad for a guy who lived out of his car and had to bathe in gas station restrooms.

Figure out what it is that can stir your blood. Discover what it is inside you that can create that white heat of passion in your life. Write down everything that you can imagine being possible for your life. Put down *everything* you could possibly want. To the side, give yourself a deadline for each item.

Some of your dreams may be extremely ambitious. You may not even believe you can achieve them now. But the simple act of putting them on paper will open up the possibilities for you to make them a reality. I can remember when I created my dream list and had no clue whatsoever how I was going to achieve those dreams. Now, just a few years later, I'm astonished by how many of those dreams have actually been realized.

Dream *big* dreams, and use those dreams to fuel your passion. Make a conscious decision to fuel your passion at every possible opportunity, and believe wholeheartedly that your dreams *can* become a reality. Success is sure to follow.

About the Author

Matt Morris is the international best-selling author of The Unemployed Millionaire. A serial entrepreneur since the age of 18, Matt has generated tens of millions of dollars through his companies while generating over 100,000 customers in 180 countries around the world. As a dynamic speaker, best-selling author, and young success story, Matt has been featured on international radio and television and has addressed audiences in over 20 countries worldwide. Matt is widely known as one of the top Internet marketing experts and is the founder of Success You Publishing, Inc.

Chapter 4

Poetry of Love

TERRI SCARBOROUGH

I have spent the last 30 days trying to decide how to condense 52 years of wisdom and leadership into 30 pages. How do I condense 32 years of being a skilled mother with patience into 30 pages. What one subject says it all? Everyone asked "What are you going to write about?" Decisions, decisions. How many times in life do we start over?

Where do you begin when you want to inspire someone? How do you get people to listen to you? What can I do to help motivate people? Why me?

Multiple Streams of Determination

All tough questions with tough choices. I try and live my life every day as if it were the best day of my life. I like to believe that friends are friends forever, and family is family, and yes the two can be the same. The best way to help someone is to listen. It's not always in your time but in God's time.

Listen

Before I go too far let me share a little with you about myself. Born the oldest of 3 children, my dad was in the military. Every 18 months we were moving around. Sometimes back to my home town in Texas and sometimes far away. I learned to make friends rather quickly and developed a few relationships that I still have today.

During our military time I lived a while in Germany and it opened my eyes to the wonders of traveling. I had the privilege to visit the standard tourist sites and historical sites through school programs and family outings. It was my introduction to foreign language. I had a knack, and a fairly quick understanding of it, mostly by listening. It is a fine art and a very useful tool. It is amazing how you can hear inflections and words in foreign languages and know what someone is actually saying if you only listen.

Team Work

My mother was the baby of 10 children and I learned at an early age what can get accomplished through the power of team work. Even until this day she is close with the remaining brothers and sisters. Through the years I watched my grandparents grow old and love each other until the end. As we traveled every other year my mother always managed to help us in packing, throwing out things I thought I couldn't live without and starting all over again. Love is the poetry of life.

Dream Big

As the early years went by, I ended up living in Alaska and graduating from high school. I learned a lot about survival there. Not just the wilderness type of survival, but about living. I married at 17 and was thrown into a world all new to me, that of being an adult. That is a lesson all in its own and should be a class taught in high school.

In the next two years I did some growing up. We made a few excursions across the state, and at one point, I found myself on top of a mountain where I was absolutely certain that no man had ever been before. It was enlightening, awe inspiring and probably the beginning of what for me was to be the changing point in my life. I was about to begin dreaming big.

Listen

I ended up back in Texas where my family was and 3 children later found myself a newly single mother with no higher education and no means of support. It was certainly time to dig in the trenches. Working nights and being a mom during the day can take its toll on anyone but somehow I managed. Then God opened up the heavens and said "Here! This is your soul mate." I met my husband, Ricky. I think God forgot to tell him for a couple of weeks but it has been a love story ever since. Poetry.

Team Work

Then there were three more children, plus two adopted children, and another baby, bringing our growing family to a total of nine. We did things in shifts, by the clock, without clocks, sometimes without knowing what day of the week it was. This is by far the biggest team work effort I feel I ever accomplished or will ever accomplish again perhaps. We have been so blessed with our family. Each one of our children has a different gift and in each one of them I see an aspect or trait of myself. They are my team.

Dream Big

In the early years of our marriage, with my ever dreaming husband we started a business that would grow into what we believe is our little empire. I like to refer to my children and the many businesses as my dynasty. We have been self employed now for almost 30 years and truly understand the dynamics of the power of prayer, the rules of fair trade, and mostly about hard work and never loosing the dream. The dream still continues and it must. You must always have goals to reach for, changes to be made, and be able to adapt to the future.

As a Mom, I wanted to stay at home and be with the children so I never had to have a job. But, with that many mouths to feed there was a need for some additional income. I started selling crafts in a booth I rented for a while. That was good around the holidays but during the off months, not so good.

We were living in Arlington, Texas and had the great idea of expanding our insulation business. Well, for anyone that works in construction business, it is not always about what you know, but who you know. We knew nobody there. Work actually picked back up in our home town so after our lease expired we moved back. That was a long two years of team work though.

Ricky would drive back and forth every weekend just so we could see each other for a few days. During this time, I was pregnant with our sixth child, living six hours away from my husband, taking care of five kids. After the birth of that child we had started the adoption process of our two other children.

Needless to say it required a lot of effort on everyone's part. We moved back to Orange, our home. To a two-bedroom house with one bathroom and a lot of love. Well as fate would have it, I was pregnant. Number Nine. We made a few adjustments, started decking in the attic of the old house and put in five bedrooms upstairs. Once again, it required team work.

Katie came into our lives on Thanksgiving morning. What a blessing.

I still needed a job. I started learning the "ins and outs" of the auction business and became a licensed auctioneer. We ran an antique auction for about seven years. When it got to the point that it was more business and time consuming than fun, it had to go.

Listen

It was at this time in my life that I became involved with young adult ministry. I took on the role of Youth Minister for the high school kids in our local parish. This was one of the most fulfilling unpaid jobs I have ever had outside being a mother.

I learned more about the fine art of listening during this time of my life than all other years combined. There are so many stories young people can tell and share with you and that they need to share. A lot of young people truly have no one that will listen to them.

Our group went from about 13 to 75 in less than a year's time. It was phenomenal. I got so much from sharing the word of God, developing friendships, and going on retreats with these young people. It will always be a highlight of my life. However, when dealing with young people there are always older people as well;

Multiple Streams of Determination

and I think Satan was working overtime to destroy the very heart of what had been created.

My life was almost destroyed by all the negativity and the politics of church and ill-meaning and miss-guided people. I never lost my faith, but my ability to trust and lead was shattered. It was at this time that I asked God to listen to me. I needed healing and understanding. So in the quite of my own heart and space, I waited and I listened and heard. Love is the poetry of life.

Team Work

The next phase of my life brought a Christian gift and book shop that I owned and operated for about six years. It was a peaceful time for me. It was very inspiring to work there and it satisfied a lot of need in me as well as the community. Some of my kids worked there and we managed it by team effort.

Then along came the beginning of the hurricanes. When Rita hit us, it ripped off ceilings and destroyed inventory, but more tragically it destroyed lives. Things were never the same again. There was no one to work, and so much reconstruction going on, there was no time for the store. So we closed. The community came together and rebuilt our town. Team work. Then a few years later Ike came and destroyed much of us again. Another community effort and much team work to put us together again.

Listen

During all the turmoil, God blessed us with a beautiful new home. We find ourselves now with only three children left at home. A few have gone on to graduate from college, one did time in the Marines and participated in the war effort. One or two got separated from the flock as sheep often do, but some have made it back home. We have three beautiful grandchildren now and a future that is brighter than ever.

Many days I like to sit and reflect on all the many lives that I have lived. I feel like reincarnation happens many times in our solitary life. The many places I have been and the things I have seen. The people I knew and the ones I hold dear as friends. It is just about listening to the person deep inside your heart.

When you are in the midst of a group, listen. You will hear what people need most. If you are making a presentation, listen then too. You will hear what they are needing you to say.

With our new adventure in the travel industry I find it is fulfilling on so many levels. It gives us the added income that I have always found to be necessary for our family. It enables me to meet new people all the time and listen to what it is they are wanting from life. It gives me big dreams. I have been able to help people with their dreams, too, and that is most rewarding.

It is not so much as getting people to listen as it is to listen. Always dream big. When you cease to dream you cease to live. Anything can be achieved with a combined effort. It takes so little time to do something bigger and better if you are doing it as a team, even if it is a team of two.

More teachers attain great wisdom by listening rather than speaking. They inspire people to dream big thoughts and plans by listening to what their hearts desire. Life is so much better when you work it as a team with loved ones.

Listen – Participate in Team Work – Inspire People to Dream Big

About the Author

Born in Texas and raised all over the world in a military family. Mother of 9 children, 3 grandchildren and a passion for traveling and loving my family. I hope to inspire many people with the power of the word. God has blessed me richly, I have overcome many diversities throughout my life.

Self-employed contractor, Youth Director, Christian book & gift store owner, Vacation Travel Specialist, and Auctioneer include the many lives that I have lived and still strive for more every day. I love to be around people, photography hobbies and scrapbooking. I love throwing parties and cooking for everyone seems to be at the top of my list.

My education comes from years of living and doing. I have taken many extra classes for the benefit of my businesses, licensing, and own personal interest. Many certifications have come my way but the broadest education I find is in living life to the fullest and never being afraid to try something new.

Terri Scarborough

409-882-4786

www.scarboroughtravel.worldventures.biz

www.terrivacations.com

www.arborenergysolutions.com

www.insulationindustries.com

tscarborough@gt.rr.com

Chapter 5

Defining Moments

MARC ACCETTA

As people of the world, we are all so different, and then again, we are all the same. While the country of our birth will have an effect on the language that we speak, the politics that we believe in, and our concept of God, we are still all just humans, who deal with pretty much the same challenges and have the same basic needs.

In most every person's life we will have what is called a defining moment, a moment of truth, where we are placed in a difficult situation, where someone or something creates a dilemma that causes us to make a choice. Normally we are faced with a choice to be disappointed or depressed, which causes us to develop a victim mentality, or to get angry and intense, which causes us to develop a fighters mentality.

Multiple Streams of Determination

Sometimes these moments come in our early childhood, before it is fair for us to be faced with such a major turn of events to deal with, and sometimes it happens in our later years. The reality is that they happen all the time. There is no rhyme or reason as to when they occur, and they may well present themselves into our lives on multiple occasions. How we respond to these moments will have a great deal to do with where we end up in life. Our lives are filled with millions of minutes that have little impact on us in the grand scheme of things, but these defining moments, although rare and brief, have a profound impact on the remaining millions of minutes that we will live.

The first defining moment that I recall was when I was playing Little League baseball. I was a pretty natural athlete, but I was not by any means a superstar in any of the sports I played, at least not until my final year of eligibility of Little League baseball. I enjoyed almost any sport, but baseball was my undeniable favorite. I spent hundreds of hours throwing a ball against the brick wall of our house (much to my father's chagrin as I would often miss the brick and hit the wood) and swinging a bat in our living room while watching baseball on TV most every evening. I would not swing the bat for a few moments here and there. I did it throughout the entire game. It was the same thing with throwing the ball against the house. I would do it for four to five hours at a time.

I spent an additional lifetime having my dad stand at point blank range and throw mini-wiffle golf balls at me, as I tried to hit them with a baseball bat, to improve my hand-eye coordination, and my bat speed. Let's just say I was "into it." I did all of this in preparation for a huge year in Little League.

I am happy to say that all of my hard work paid off in a big way. I led my team with a .575 batting average and led the league in home runs. I did all of that without ever striking out the entire year. I also went

Defining Moments

all year at my first base position with only one fielding error. I was incredibly proud of what I had achieved. To top it all off, our team, the Bearcats, won our second consecutive league championship.

Only one thing could make this fairytale season even better -- to be a star on the All-Star team. The very best players from the regular season get selected to try out for the All-Stars. The All-Star team is the one that competes with other leagues and states and eventually can earn their way to the Little League World Series in Williamsport, N.Y. That was my ultimate objective, to be the star first baseman on the world championship team.

The two days of tryouts went as expected. There were two other guys trying out for first base, but neither of them had an outstanding year, and neither of them did anything overly impressive in tryouts. I continued the successful play that I had displayed all year. My confidence was at an all-time high.

When we broke tryouts and I made the team, it was exciting, but expected. I was having fun getting to know all my new teammates. It was so exciting to see my dreams unfolding right in front of my eyes. We were to begin practice as a team the following Saturday.

This is where the story takes a very tragic twist. When our coaches called out the first string team to take the field for the initial scrimmage, I was not called out to play first base. They called out a guy named Scott (who had hit .250 with no homeruns in the regular season). I was in a state of shock that Scott even made the team.

I sat on the bench in a state of shock. How was this possible? I don't remember anything that happened the rest of the practice. When it was over, my father (a loud Italian from New York City who always wore his heart on his sleeve) pulled the coaches aside and had a heated

Multiple Streams of Determination

discussion. One of the coaches was my coach on the Bearcats, Mr. Romyns, and the other coach was the coach of our archrivals, the Tigers.

Mr. Dalbagno was Scott's coach on the Tigers. Scott's dad, unbeknownst to me, was a local businessman who had a tremendous amount of pull with the league founders, and was apparently a financial backer for the whole league. When my father got into the car, he was seething. Four letter words were streaming out of his mouth, mostly in Italian. He proceeded to tell me that they explained to him that Scott was a better defensive player, and that he would be the starting first baseman for the good of the team.

I was crushed. I was experiencing outrage for the first time in my 12 years on the planet. This was so unjust! What a joke! And the worst part was that there was nothing I could do about it. I had done everything right. I was on the verge of living out my dreams, dreams that I had earned the hard way, but now they were slipping down the drain right in front of my eyes.

The next few days were a blur. I shed a huge number of tears and my father screamed to anyone who would listen. When it came time for our next practice, my dad told me that, if I decided to quit the team, he would fully support me. This was a big deal because he had always instilled into me that I should never quit anything that I had begun – ever.

There was a part of me that wanted to just lay in bed and quit, especially with my father's blessing, but there was a bigger part of me that made me get up, get dressed, and get on my bike to ride down the hill to practice.

This was my earliest defining moment that I can recall. At the time, I had no idea that it was happening. Just the same, it was definitely a

Defining Moments

defining moment. I took my place with the team and started playing catch with my buddy Mike. I was fighting back tears with everything that I had in me. As the practice went on, I got better control of my emotions, but it was a very tough two hours.

I just would not let these men and the decisions that they made, that I did not understand or agree with, make me quit the game I loved. Several of my teammates pulled me aside and told me what a raw deal I was getting. That made me feel better, but it was a consolation prize as it was apparent I would be on the bench for the biggest games of my life.

The funny thing is that Scott seemed oblivious to what was going on. He didn't even seem to realize the absurd politics that had him playing and me sitting. Scott was actually a really nice kid and over the years we became friends, as good of friends as we could be given the awkward situation.

I was a bit sullen over the days leading up to our first game, but I refused to let anyone see the gut-wrenching turmoil that I was experiencing inside. Game day came on a bright Saturday morning in July. I was usually so excited on game day that I would wake up when it was still dark out and be filled with electricity until the first pitch of the game was thrown.

Today was different. I lay in bed for hours before I got up at the last moment I could to still arrive on time. I was still crushed, but I was determined to be a good teammate and leave my personal sadness at home. The stands were packed. It seemed like the whole town was there.

I went through the motions of warming up and taking batting practice, but for the first time in my life, it seemed pointless. And then the game

Multiple Streams of Determination

began. It was so surreal, but it was happening. I got on my feet and routed our pitcher Sam on with the loudest voice I could muster.

We played great that game. Sam threw a one hitter and we scored about 10 runs. I got to pinch hit in the last inning and ripped a double to left field, driving in two runs. It was good, but it was also empty and meaningless because the game was already decided. My teammates were all over me when I got back to the dugout. All in all, I had survived.

The next Tuesday at practice, I happened to overhear the coaches talking about their concern that we were playing one of the toughest teams in the state, and that they aware that Scott was the only starter who had not gotten a hit in our thrilling victory on Saturday. My coach recommended starting me, but he was quickly shot down. They instructed him to tell me to "be ready" in case they needed me at a crucial moment.

I went into that game with a better feeling of self worth, but that seemed to wither as the game wore on and I was still riding the pine. That team was great and we were down 2-0 after the fifth inning. The tournament we were in was a one loss elimination format, so if we lost we were done. In Little League, we only play six innings, so the pressure was on.

In our half of the sixth inning, we got two men on base, but we were down to our last out. Just as if we were in a movie, Scott was the hitter who was due up for us. As he strode toward home plate, our coach called him back and told me to grab a bat. I was about to pinch hit with the game, and with it our season, on the line.

I was so excited that I could not breathe. I stepped up to the plate feeling certain I would drill the ball and win the game. That feeling disappeared quickly as their pitcher blew a fast ball by me with more velocity that I had ever experienced.

Defining Moments

I went from excited and confident to intense in the bat of an eye. I stepped out of the batter's box and composed myself. I knew the pitcher wanted to get this game over with, and he knew that he had just thrown the ball right by me, so I prepared myself for another fastball right down the pipe.

That is exactly what he threw. Much to my amazement, I ripped the ball into the right center field gap. I put my head down and ran as fast as I could. I ended up diving into third base with a triple. I had tied the game! Our fans were going crazy. It was the greatest feeling of my life up to that point. The next batter got another hit and I scored the go-ahead run. As I went out to my rightful first base position, with our team ahead 3-2, I was filled with so much pride and satisfaction. Not because I had gotten the hit and proven the coaches wrong, but because I had not quit.

That may be a rather adult perspective for a 12 year old to have, but I vividly remember having that feeling very strongly. I had faced my defining moment and I had won. So much of me was destroyed. So much of me was feeling how unfair the whole situation was. So much of me felt betrayed, but I did not quit.

Only years later, when I started to take inventory of my past experiences, did I realize just how meaningful that moment was. The late, great Green Bay Packers legendary coach Vince Lombardi said, "Winning is a habit. Unfortunately, so is losing." I had started to create the habit of hanging in there in tough times at 12, under what seemed to me, to be the worst circumstance imaginable.

I can honestly tell you several decades later, having been blessed to achieve a great deal of financial success, that my greatest skill is not giving up. I have never been the smartest, or the strongest, or the most

Multiple Streams of Determination

skilled, but I do stay the course. I have discovered that in virtually every area of life that we will win if we just keep going.

I wish I could tell you that we won the Little League World Series that year and that I was the star of the team, but that would not be the truth. The leadoff hitter for the opposing team got a single, and the second hitter drilled a homerun, and just like that, our season was over.

It was a bittersweet moment for me. I was very happy with what I had overcome and achieved, but heartbroken that we had lost and my dreams of getting to the World Series were over. Our bus ride home was dead silent. When we got back to our home field and disbanded into our parents' cars, virtually all of my teammates made a point of congratulating me.

As I drove home that evening, and even now as I recall these events, I had a feeling of peace and gratitude. I had been dealt some nasty circumstances, and was able to fight through them. I now realize that that day my dad gave me the option of giving up was my first true defining moment. Year later, while watching one of my favorite actors (Kevin Costner) in one of my favorite movies (Tin Cup) he made a statement that says it best.

His character faces a crucial moment in the movie and emerges victorious. Costner tells his afterward tells his buddy that, when life gives you a defining moment, "Either you define the moment, or the moment defines you."

Whether you are young or more mature, whether you are male or female, whether you are educated of uneducated, whether you are born wealthy or poor, whether you are spiritual or an atheist, you will deal with defining moments.

Perhaps you will be like I was in this story and not even realize what is happening as these moments occur, or perhaps my story will help you be fully aware of what is happening. In any event, these are the key moments in our lives. Make no mistake about it. These are the moments that will shape your destiny.

Life is not always fair, but the truth is that it does not need to be. It is not the cards we are dealt that matters as much as the way that we play those cards. In *Man's Search for Meaning*, the author Victor Frankl clearly illustrates that we cannot control what happens to us, but we have absolute control over how we respond to what happens to us.

Be prepared for life's curveballs, and just like I was fortunate enough to do so many years ago, drill the ball that you are thrown into the gap and define the moment.

About the Author

When Marc graduated Seton Hall University in 1982 with a degree in Political Science, he had no idea what direction his life would take. He entered the world of sales at the urging of a friend named Gary. Marc did not feel he would be very successful in that world but decided it a shot since he had no other lucrative opportunities. A little over thirty years later, Marc has excelled at every sales related business he has ventured into. From direct selling, to recruitment, to management, and ultimately training, Marc has put together an overwhelmingly successful resume of achievements.

Marc is currently the Founder of MarcAccettaSeminars and the Director of Training for the explosive internet based Travel Company of WorldVentures. Marc addresses live audiences every month where he impacts tens of thousands of lives every year. Marc also produces a wide variety of CD's and DVD's and is working on the completion of his next book.

Multiple Streams of Determination

Marc was initially a student of all he now teaches. Marc says, "I did not grow up with a high level of self confidence or self esteem." He attended dozens of live seminars over the last 30 years, has read hundreds of books, and has studied many highly successful people. "I had a burning desire to improve in any way I could, in all areas of my life." Marc took the information and put it into *action*. That action started to yield results. As the results started to mount up, his self esteem and self confidence increased with them. Ultimately, Marc developed a passion for teaching everything that he had learned over the years. "I realized that achieving success in my own life was not enough for me." Marc derives his greatest joy from teaching what his life studies have taught him to others.

Marc shares his passions with many people through his live seminars and coaching programs, but he also speaks at schools and youth organizations whenever his schedule allows for it. He and his wife Kelly became active members of Big Brother Big Sister in 2004. Their experience with their *little brother* William inspired them to become even more involved with the organization. They inspired many others to become Big Brothers and Sisters and ultimately were asked to head up the local Board of Directors for BBBS.

The success they have enjoyed with BBBS has inspired them to found their *Unstoppable Foundation* which will teach many of the life skills he shares with business people with middle school aged children. Marc and Kelly feel very fortunate that they have found the keys to success for their own lives and will undoubtedly spend the rest of their life teaching them to others.

Chapter 6

Why Ask "Why"?

YVETTE SHAW

If we could repeat any of the painful challenges we have encountered in our lives, it would be my guess that most of them would not be experiences we would reiterate, regardless of the wisdom and inner growth we had gained. Depending on our mindset, these attributes are not necessarily worthy of the painful price.

Although pain is an emotion we usually try our very best to avoid, there are some occasions when we are willing to experience this feeling repeatedly because we are aware from the outset the benefits we stand to gain. These occasions include childbirth, medical and cosmetic surgery, resistance training, running a marathon as well as others.

Multiple Streams of Determination

Embarking on a journey of self-development, self-discovery and recovery is one that will always be painful in both negative and positive ways. There will be many twists and turns with the changes of terrain. However, continually reinventing and applying ourselves will enable us to realize our purpose-driven lives.

I wrote this chapter especially to inspire and encourage those who have a family member with a disability or know of someone who has one. Other than disabilities that result from accidents, some of the genetic/hereditary and biological factors associated with specific disorders such as autism unfortunately continue to prevent the medical profession from determining the exact underlying cause.

Depending on its severity, a physical disability can hugely affect one's independence. In this case, great turmoil can be experienced, especially as the person struggles to come to terms with the situation. A neurological disorder or mental illness resulting from the factors previously mentioned can create terrible uncertainty and dysfunction, not only for the individual concerned but also for the immediate family and friends.

Following the birth of my son, I was extremely overjoyed. Being in my mid-twenties and naturally ambitious and successful, I was excited as the highs and lows of parenting were about to reveal themselves.

Unfortunately, however, with no highs anywhere in sight, my world came crashing down when I was informed after six months that my son was diagnosed with a condition called global developmental delay. His special needs would increase over the forthcoming years, and as predicted, they did. He was later diagnosed with autistic spectrum disorder (ASD) together with complex learning difficulties, challenging behavior, hyperkinetic disorder (a severe form of attention deficit hyperactivity disorder (ADHD)), verbal dyspraxia

Why Ask "Why"?

(significant speech disorder), epilepsy and mild microlissencephaly (a lesser form of brain malfunction).

After receiving this news, the frightening reality of providing a lifetime of care for someone with a disability was hugely difficult to digest and accept. It resonated even deeper as I painfully struggled to come to terms with who that someone actually was – my only child!

Whilst I tried to focus on my glass being half full in the presence of family, friends and those in the medical field, the harsh reality was that I silently felt it was empty.

Have you ever experienced an overwhelming feeling of guilt that tore away at your soul? I should have been satisfied and grateful my son was alive, but secretly I wanted more. Although I loved him passionately and we had an inseparable bond, at times I battled with my emotions. I wanted a different child, one who was meeting his milestones so my self-worth would return.

How many of us are guilty of wasting valuable time each day wishing our lives were different? We are constantly told to change our situation if we do not like it. Being a driven and self-motivated individual, I had always been successful in accomplishing my personal dreams and goals. Planning for a brighter tomorrow was always a major part of enjoying today.

Suddenly I was in bereavement, and today started to be the tomorrow I worried about yesterday. It is said that you cannot miss what you have never had. However, I found myself missing what I thought I was going to have.

Losing a loved one in our lives can be devastating. Whether the loss is derived from the person dying or from watching the quality of the

Multiple Streams of Determination

individual's life deteriorate significantly due to ill health or a disability, we inevitably go through a mourning process.

Families affected by autism often feel as though they are mourning a loss, especially if the diagnosis was made following a vaccination. Usually the mother devotes considerably more time to that child, and in so doing, her spouse and/or other children are often deprived of love and attention. Marriages sometimes break up as positive communication ceases and negative emotions are expressed. Individual identities are often lost as family members struggle to understand and come to terms with their personal devastation.

My grief was so overwhelming that I lost a large part of my identity for many years. I was consumed with finding the answers to my son's problems. I read religiously on a number of topics relating to his disabilities, always seeking to find the underlying cause and to discover new information. We attended every medical assessment looking for more clues and more answers. I insisted on getting him as much assistance as possible in school, after school, on weekends and during the school holidays.

The reality, however, was that a few hours of respite here and there were not enough. I was burnt out. Masking my own inadequacies and fears of how I would be perceived if I asked for additional help was torturous. I have since learned, however, that the crosses we fear are much heavier to carry than the ones we bear.

Caring for someone with autistic tendencies, challenging behavior and severe hyperactivity was a mighty task, especially if specific behavioral control strategies were not implemented. Even though I loved my son dearly, I disliked his behavior immensely and had to make a concerted effort to separate these two very distinct feelings.

Why Ask "Why"?

Standing on the periphery of my son's autistic world was bewildering. I often studied his restricted and repetitive behavior with amazement. A long-term developmental disability that impairs social interaction and communication was, in my opinion, incarceration at its very worst. Being the target of his unprovoked physical and verbal attacks was a common feature in our lives. Dealing with his general defiance and inappropriate bouts of loud and unwarranted laughter became increasingly difficult. His speech impediment was a further major source of frustration for us both as he struggled to communicate his needs and wants effectively.

Being able to communicate for oneself is such a precious gift. What if we lost our voices today? What if we could no longer communicate our wants and needs tomorrow? How would others perceive us and how would we define ourselves? What would we do to reclaim our dignity and acceptance in society? How would we deal with our own frustrations?

My relationship with God had suffered considerably. At times, I wanted nothing to do with Him. After all, He had not been there for me, or so it seemed! I just could not understand what terrible sin I could possibly have committed to warrant this life sentence. After going around the same mountain relentlessly with the same questions being unanswered, a very close friend explained how truly merciful God in fact was. He relayed how He had been by my side continually throughout my entire journey, and how God had actually graciously carried my weary soul when I was too tired to go on.

It was then that I truly decided to relent and ask God to inspire me to reconnect with myself and develop a new relationship with Him. We all want to have a clear direction, but ultimately, God has the master plan for our lives. Although I knew the transition would be slow, I

Multiple Streams of Determination

decided to change direction and climb the mountain instead of circling it, so I could eventually see the view.

Feeling broken and helpless enabled me to finally accept that I could not care for my son all by myself and admit that I did not want to look after him on my own, either. I deserved to be happy and fulfilled, and my son deserved to be given the opportunity to be and to do his very best.

My devastation sparked the beginning of a radical body transformation for me, both internally and externally. I started to channel my negative energy and fears into resistance and cardiovascular training almost daily. Heavy weight training sessions and vigorous cardiovascular exercise were the two modalities that strengthened my mind and body, releasing my toxic thoughts and feelings. I was now being prepared spiritually for the long and challenging emotional journey ahead.

As a personal trainer, I believed every workout at the gym had to count for something and be more challenging than the previous one. I found solace in my training regimen and listened to many gospel tracks to lift my spirit. Although anti-depressants had been prescribed, I wanted to travel this road without stimulants. I was fully aware of the cause of my depression and knew that drugs would not relieve the symptoms. My body was a precious temple of God, and in order to be healed, I needed to accept and work through my emotions instead of suppressing them. My temple was ready to be spiritually fed and cleansed. God had become my training buddy, and whenever I felt I was lacking in strength, I would meditate on His word to infuse me with some of His.

Over time, as the intensity of my workouts increased, I gradually started to feel a sense of divine peace. The urge to exercise was so profound that I did so without actually knowing or caring why. God had placed

Why Ask "Why"?

a huge calling on my heart, and although I did not understand the implications of this for a number of years, part of my assignment was later revealed in my divinely sculptured physique. I am now a professional international body builder!

They say that muscles are made as much in the kitchen as they are in the gym. However, they only grow when the corresponding muscle fibers are significantly broken down, warranting nutrients and recuperation for repair and growth. The intense pain felt that kick-starts this process is known as "the burn" and signifies being broken down - the perfect condition for muscle tissue to grow in. Consequently, if you keep on breaking down the tissue before it has had a chance to recuperate, your training will become counterproductive as the size and strength of your muscles decrease.

To a degree, this is the same in our everyday lives. At certain painful times, unless we too are significantly broken down, change and growth will not take effect. However, unlike our muscles, which require the burn to progress, burn-out in our lives will ensure regression until we decide to change.

Even though I had been disappointed that life had not met my own expectations, with hindsight I now feel fulfilled when I reflect on how my determination to help those who are "less able" has had a significant impact, not only on their lives but also on mine.

On one particular occasion, I was the host of a mainstream television documentary where I revealed the government's intention to close a number of special-needs schools for children with learning disabilities. The rationale was that integration with mainstream students would be beneficial for all pupils. Now whilst that conclusion may have been true for some students with moderate learning difficulties, those with severe or complex learning disabilities would have found it extremely difficult to integrate, and some would not have managed it at all. The media coverage generated enabled my son's day school to remain open.

After many years, however, it became apparent that his school was failing his needs. With the help of an attorney who truly believed in us, a judicial decision was enforced against the local educational authority. My son was granted a residential school placement when he was nine years old, and since then he has continued to receive a modified educational program together with twenty-four hours of personal care as and when required. Now living a quality assisted life, he is able to contribute to society and live on his own terms. He has been afforded the opportunity to be the best that he can be.

As mentioned earlier in this chapter, we often waste so much time lamenting how things used to be or how we would like things to be that we miss the new opportunities and experiences that flow toward us. It is said that all you need is the right person to believe in you to make a difference in your life. As with everything, faith is the key that allows new doors to be opened.

You cannot heal the wounds you do not feel, and so you have not really lived until you have done something for someone who can never repay you.

About the Author

Yvette Shaw's portfolio of success has been accomplished by her achievements as an International Lifestyle and Fitness Expert. She is a Certified Personal Trainer and Nutrition Specialist, Emotional Freedom Technique (EFT) Practitioner, Certified Make-Up Artist, Actress, International Physique and Muscle Model (Professional), Entrepreneur and Mentor.

Applying healthy nutrition, cutting-edge exercise and positive behaviour changes to her Lifestyle programs has enabled Yvette's clients to become their own personal engineers of life. Her lean, sculptured physique is the epitome of her product as she believes that whilst 'getting older is inevitable, feeling older is optional'.

Able to think 'outside of the box', Yvette challenges values and beliefs that are no longer serving the individual so that a new set of beliefs and positive behaviours can emerge without actually 'reinventing the wheel'.

She is an inspiration to people from various walks of life, especially women, single parents and those who are considered as 'under-achievers', due to emotional, neurological and/or physical disability. Yvette continues to empower and encourage those who cross her path to step forward along their own paths to recovery and self-discovery, thus creating a space where they can live their dreams and experience transformation.

www.yvetteshaw.com

info@yvetteshaw.com

Chapter 7

Don't Sleep Through Your Wake Up Call

TERRY ELLISON

Are you currently awake in your life? Do you feel that you are living up to your full potential? If I asked you to paint a clear picture of what your ultimate life would look like, could you do it? Have you ever even thought about it? The funny thing is that the vast majority of humans would answer "no" to each of those simple questions. How could that be the case?

The fact is most humans are sleep-walking through life. What's even scarier is that those same people may never wake up. They will never even realize the enormous power they possess within. This power could catapult them into their full potential in life.

Multiple Streams of Determination

Chances are you don't know my story, yet. I was raised in an upper middle class family with enormous love and support. I was never fed with a silver spoon but I did enjoy other things that most kids did not. I was taught the value of hard work and to always give 100 percent. Believe it or not, I was even told I could achieve anything I wanted in life. I have always been a very driven, positive person.

Why, then, did it take me until June 2008 to wake up? Until that particular month I had not experienced what is usually critical to all who become ultra-successful in life. I'm talking about extreme pain and humiliation. In a nutshell, my happy family was disrupted, a person I passionately cared for did not return the favor, and I almost paid a visit to my grave. No really, I survived an awful accident, which led to my waking point.

I want to impress upon you three things that can drastically change your chance for success. If you ever want to achieve your full potential, then you will have to master all three.

Opening Your Eyes

Among the most important things is you must open your eyes. You have to wake up and leave your ordinary Joe status. You have to understand that you have a greater purpose. I promise you aren't meant to be ordinary and unhappy. You were put here to thrive in life. So wake up! Do it now.

After my accident, I quickly realized that tomorrow is not promised. Many of you have had close calls before. Maybe a friend or relative has experienced a huge scare. Possibly you've been a witness to much worse things. Anybody knows that you only get one chance to live your life. Therefore, you had better not currently be on a test run like most people.

Don't Sleep Through Your Wake Up Call

The brilliant French essayist Michel Eqyuem de Montaigne says it perfectly. "The value of life lies not in the length of days, but in the use we make of them; a man may live long yet live very little." If that quote doesn't send chills through your spine then you are still asleep in life.

I want you to start paying attention to people when you go out into the world each day. Plenty of people will appear happy. But inside the core of most humans is frustration. Those same people you see having a great time at lunch will be angry two hours later at their spouse. Their boss has stressed them overboard or their children are misbehaving at school. This is what I call the Robot Cycle. People are stuck in jobs they hate, working for corporations that could care less about them. They fear starting their own company and claim they are just too busy. Is this you? Are you a robot human? Do you live paycheck to paycheck or are you building your wealth doing something you love? Chances are you are like 90 percent of the population, stuck in the same robot cycle each day.

If this describes your life and you are beyond sick of that pain, then you need to make an immediate change. Realize that which you are currently doing will not get you to your dream life. Starting today you need to figure out your true passions. What is it that really fires you up? Then you need a game plan to attack that passion with a vengeance. Believe me, inside of you lies the power to become ultra successful if your desire is big enough to pursue your passion.

The Number One thing to do if you want to make a huge change in your life is to take absolute, 100 percent responsibility for your outcome. When I learned this, my life changed. Stop blaming your boss, the economy, or whatever false excuse you have for your current situation. You are now responsible for your life, one you have complete control over. Did I mention also that you will now be eliminating all fear, worry, and negativity as well? These are killers to your success in anything and you must master the extermination of these.

So now that you have total control of your life, you are awake and motivated, positive and strong, let's move on to the next phase of the game.

Think and Dream Big

It's time for you to think and dream big. We all know that you are what you think about most. The mind is the most powerful tool you have. It is imperative that you learn how to use it properly. You must control your thoughts if you want to win big.

Donald Trump says you have to think anyway, so why not think big? You have to know that your dreams can be your reality. What business have you always wanted to start? What countries have you always wanted to take your family to? You can absolutely achieve any of this if you believe it and never quit. I'm telling you right now this is a fact. I've marked off six of my bucket list items in the past year all because I've done the previous things discussed. I dream big! Scratch that, I dream huge!

Your new attitude will bring great challenges. You now speak a totally different language than the majority of the world. You are going to have people close to you who are negative. Never let them steal your dream. If those close to you won't support you, then you have to prove them wrong until they do.

It is critical that you start thinking outside of your own self. What do I mean by that? The fact is that most people only see their world clearly. Think about that for a minute. If you are starting a business only for yourself, this is a problem. If you are so tied up in what your family has going on and care little about anyone else, this is a major problem. You will absolutely need the help of others to achieve your greatness. Who would want to help someone who has only one agenda, that being their own? This is going to hold you back if you don't leave your little Island now and start connecting with the world of others. Big picture thinkers dream big and see a world different from their own. No, everything isn't all about you and your happiness. Actually, if you want to be super successful, then you had better make it about others more than yourself. It's a proven fact that by helping more people get what they want, the more you will get what you want. So help others first then watch a new world open up that you didn't know existed. Good things will just flow to you in abundance.

Take Massive Action

Now that you are awake and dreaming big it's time to take action. I mean massive consistent action. If you aren't prepared to go all in then you will not achieve the massive success that determination can bring. You will have to sacrifice and go through pain in order to reach the mountain top. Nothing worth having comes without pain. According to the Marines, pain is weakness leaving the body. Never run from pain because it is necessary to make real success possible.

As Les Brown would say, it's time to step into your greatness. As we discussed before, you have total greatness deep inside of you. If you want to unleash this power within, you must wake up, dream big, and take massive action. You have to do this now as soon as you have your true passion figured out. Don't wait; the time will never be perfect. One of the most powerful concepts I have learned is to act even when the path is unclear. T Harv Ecker, one of the best success trainers in the world, has a powerful saying: "Ready, shoot, aim." Think about that for a minute and how you can use it to pursue your passion in life.

Your Time is Now

I want you to realize that at the time this book is released, you are in one of the best economies there may ever be to put your plan into action. How could I be serious? I must be crazy, right? I'm dead serious when I tell you that blood is in the water. When that happens the real sharks feast. Many experts proclaim the perfect storm of opportunity is upon us. When there is fear mixed with uncertainty for the masses, real fortune is made. Just ask Warren Buffett.

How can I be so certain? Well for one, the richest man on the planet says so. If that isn't enough to convince you then look at corporate America. Ah yes, comfort and stability, right? Wrong! Corporations are draining you of your true purpose. You are a robot in their system with fear to break free. The vast majority of these companies do not care about you or your happiness. They care about themselves and their shareholders' retirement accounts. Retirement account? Do you have one, and how much has it grown in the past five years? Yeah, that's what I thought. Have you been given a performance bonus lately for all of your hard work? I recently read that corporate workers who stay in their job for five years are no more than 10 percent better at their craft than they were the second year. What this tells me is that people stop growing. They are in robot mode. The fact of the matter is that if you aren't creating more skills each year you will remain at the same level of wages going forward. Do not let that be you. Top corporate talent is being laid off or simply leaving in droves to branch out on their own. You have the chance to partner with these extremely successful people in your venture.

Simple Steps

If you are tired of your boring job and lame boss, then here is what I would do first. Visualize yourself pursuing your dreams and feel how powerful it makes you. Next, write down your top three reasons why it is imperative you reach your true potential. These reasons have to be clear and in perfect detail. Each goal you set must have a reason behind it or you won't have the courage to pursue with intensity. Once done, take immediate action. Do not worry about getting everything perfect as you can learn on the fly.

One of the best pieces of advice I got growing up was from my former football coach in middle school. He used to drill into our stubborn heads that if you want to get better you have to fail faster. You have to fail and get back up. You have to always learn from failure and get back up. Keep this principle in mind early on when roadblocks appear.

Go Make It Happen

I truly hope that you now have an idea of what your calling involves. You need to go out each day and consciously put your new thoughts into action. If you do this you will be awake and on your way to your real power. Dream big every day and remember why it is that you must reach your true potential. I was always determined to be a person of value, but until I woke up I never realized how much further I could go in life. I am now strong, I am a warrior, and I will not rest until I have reached my full potential. Use your determination and motivating desires to join me on this journey. I promise you that it is a journey you will never regret. Go and be free. It's only a couple of steps away.

About the Author

Terry Ellison is a home based business entrepreneur with a burning passion to inspire others to their full potential in life. After graduating from Texas Tech University in 2003 he led one of the Southern Regions top five ranked Insurance Agencies in sales two years running. He then moved into the banking industry and joined the ranks of top ten in sales for his tenure, twice reaching top rank company wide. He was then hired by a small business debt management firm to build out their financial & contract enrollment systems, of which would increase revenue by 1.2 million within the year.

Upon having a near brush with death Ellison's attention turned to his true calling of motivating, leading, and training others to great levels of success; a phrase he refers to as Lifestyle Optimization. His latest project, Adventure Free LLC is aimed at just that, helping people attain a true freedom lifestyle. He is an up and coming speaker & author with multiple projects in the works this year. You can learn more about Terry Ellison and his work by visiting his website below.

www.TerryEllison.me

Contact Email

terry@terryellison.me

www.Adventure-Free.com

Contact Email

info@adventure-free.com

Chapter 8

Separated To Be Elevated

JOHN DI LEMME

If you are a Champion *(you most definitely are)*, then you will be promoted to greater and higher realms of leadership. Life has a way of elevating true Champions. Just as cream rises to the top of milk, true Champions rise to the top of companies, projects, and great events. When that happens, old relationships fall away. It can be emotional and difficult, but it's part of the price of leadership. Champions must be separated from the crowd before they can be elevated into prominence.

I only hang out with Champions. My mastermind team consists wonderful, fired up, success maniacs that are striving to succeed in every area of their life. They support and encourage my "Why" in life, which is my ultimate purpose, and I support them the same way. But, you

Multiple Streams of Determination

know what? Not one of them is someone I knew from my past. Except for my parents and some family, not one of my friends from my old days is around me today. Think about that; I was separated away from the lower levels. That's not prideful talk. I'm humbled and grateful for the way that God has elevated me in life and blessed me with the ability to change the lives of others worldwide. However, I'm confident when I tell you that one of the prices that Champions have to pay is being separated from the old gang.

I won't even try to convince you that this is an easy process. Sometimes it happens naturally after you begin to immerse yourself in positive self-development materials and activities. One day you look around, and you are surrounded by positive, like-minded people. Believe me, negative naysayers don't want to hang around with someone that is always speaking empowering words or has a positive outlook on life despite the obstacles that they face.

On the other hand, sometimes those friends that are always dragging you down just decide to hang around and try harder to squash your Why in life. What do you do? You have to exercise the gift of goodbye. Explain to those people that you are on a path to success and you cannot allow them to steal your dreams. It's like a bad apple in a barrel of delicious red apples. That bad apple becomes cankerous and destroys all of the bright, vibrant apples. This is what happens when you allow those so-called friends to continually badger you with their negative nonsense.

I readily admit that I am always ready to embrace goodbye. I only spend time with Champions. Of course, I'll assist someone that is struggling to find success. I am a mentor, and I'm pretty good at spotting the Champions inside of people that are fighting to get out. You've seen them too; they're not addicted to negative attitudes and words. They are always searching the horizon in order to spot their future.

Separated to be Elevated

When they see it, they go for it. I will always have time to assist those people. I love them…Champions struggling to be born.

It is not hateful to tell someone goodbye. Rather, it's faithful. It's faithful to your own dream and to live the life of a Champion. It's not a personal thing. You shouldn't be cruel or dismissive of others, but you simply have to respond to the call of success. That call will always separate you before it elevates you. Plus you have a responsibility to yourself, your dream and your family to answer the success call that you know will forever change your life.

I have seen people elevated while trying to hang on to someone from the old days. If they continue, the old buddy will often trip them up. Not because he's a bad guy, but because he's addicted to negativity. It's like eagles trying to hang out with pigeons. There's nothing wrong with pigeons, but they will NEVER be eagles. You are an eagle! Fly higher than the pigeons and don't look down.

If you're making $50,000 a year, start hanging out with people who make $200,000 a year. Learn their secrets. Ask them to teach you. That's what "separated to be elevated" means. You make a choice about the kind of influences, the kind of people, the kind of books, the kind of movies and the kind of material that you will allow into your mind and heart. Remember, whatever goes into your eyes and ears ultimately comes out one way or the other and manifests itself in your life. Think about it. If you continue to surround yourself with negative naysayers that don't believe in you, then how on Earth can you expect to believe in yourself and your dream? There's no way that you can!

This is serious stuff. Listen to me. If you were determined to become physically fit and healthy, you wouldn't continue to stuff your cabinets full of Twinkies, donuts, beer, and Doritos. No, you would find the gift of goodbye. You would move out of the old nutritional neighbor-

Multiple Streams of Determination

hood and ban all junk food from your house. You would allow yourself to be separated from McDonalds and Pizza Hut in order to be elevated to healthy power foods. What if you tried to be healthy, but said, "I can't leave my old friends – the fries, the cakes, the milk shakes – I can't forsake them?" How long would your dream of health and physical fitness last? It's the same thing with success and living as a Champion.

You have a decision to make. Are you going to be a Champion? Are you willing to pay the price? The struggle is vitally important. It does something in you and for you. I've never known a Champion who didn't have to struggle with shaking off the old in order to embrace the new. The number of obstacles and types of adversity that you face in life will lay the foundation for massive growth. When your dream is built on a solid foundation, the only way that your level of success in life can go is up! Allow your frustration to drive you and commit to developing a strong foundation that will support your magnificent Why in life.

Let me tell you, sometimes between the separated and the elevated, there is a very lonely period. You've been separated from your old friends and not yet integrated with lots of Champions. That is a real testing time. I was in my twenties when I made the decision to leave my old friends behind. At that time, I was surrounded by many so-called friends that called me everyday to hang out. It wasn't until I began my success journey that I finally realized that I was wasting precious time by hanging out with that crowd. I wanted so much more out of life and believed I could achieve it.

Unfortunately, my friends weren't ready to step out in faith and build a new life for themselves. After a while, I noticed that the phone stopped ringing and I rarely saw any of those people. It was very lonely but I eventually met new friends that believed in me as much as I believed

Separated to be Elevated

in myself and my Why in life. Imagine that scene…a twenty four year old stuttering kid that could barely say his own name telling his friends about his dream. I was laughed at, ridiculed and told that I would never achieve that kind of success. Guess What? I proved them wrong and so can you!

If you want to achieve greatness in your life, then you have to make the decision to develop a mastermind team of positive, influential people that are success-driven and believe in you. In the beginning, they might even believe in you more than you actually believe in yourself. When you have those kind of friends, failure is not an option because they won't let you quit.

Have you ever tried to steer a parked car? Not much excitement there. It's far better to steer a car that's moving. The power steering is flowing, the tires are moving on the highway, and you can gently and effortlessly glide that vehicle right up onto the road. When you try to steer from a parked, no power, cold-engine spot on the driveway, nothing happens. Success is like that. You will never be able to turn the key in your heart and travel down the road of success without first pulling out of the old, comfortable parking spot of negative associations.

You're a Champion! Your car is already moving. The fact that you're reading this message and not a comic book or other time-waster means that your car is moving pretty well and it's ready to race down the success speedway. Just keep rolling . . . right on past the slower cars, the older cars and the beat-up pick-ups that have not been maintained. You were destined for higher elevations. It's time to go for it!

John Di Lemme

www.ChampionsLiveFree.com

About the Author

In September 2001, John Di Lemme founded Di Lemme Development Group, Inc., a company known worldwide for its role in expanding the personal development industry. As president and CEO, John strives for excellence in every area of his business and believes that you must surround yourself with a like-minded team in order to stay on top of your game.

In addition to building a successful company, John has changed lives around the globe as an international motivational speaker. Over the past eighteen years, he has shared the stage with the best of the best including Dr. John Maxwell, Dennis Waitley, Jim Rohn, Les Brown, Mark Victor Hansen and Loral Langemeier only to name a few. This is truly an amazing feat for someone that was clinically diagnosed as a stutterer at a very young age and told that he would never speak fluently.

John truly believes that everyone needs personal development to reach their full potential in life, and his determination to reach all forms of media with his motivational messages has catapulted his career. He is an accomplished author of several books including his latest best selling book, "10 Life Lessons on How to Find Your Why Now & Achieve Ultimate Success." John has also featured on many television programs and interviewed countless times. As a multi-million dollar entrepreneur, John is one of the most highly sought after strategic business coaches in the world.

John's passion is to teach others how to live a champion life despite the label that society has placed on them. Through his books, audio/video materials, sold-out live seminars, numerous television interviews, intensive training boot camps, live webinars, website (www.ChampionsLiveFree.com), podcasts and weekly tele-classes, John has made success a reality for thousands worldwide.

Chapter 9

Blueprint of a Dream

BOBBY MINOR

When I decided to write a chapter for this book, there was one thing I was adamant about. I am not going to tell you what you need to do to bring your dreams to life. Rather, I'm going to tell you what I did to bring my dreams to life.

In looking back at what I would consider major dreams I've brought to life, I find they all pretty much fall into two categories. The first category is dreams I pursued "just because." These are dreams that didn't impact or change my life or anyone else's. They were just things that I always wanted to do. Let's call these "personal dreams" or dreams of attainment. They include things like putting together my own semi-pro baseball team and winning the championship, learning to play ice hockey and being named league MVP, performing stand-up comedy and visiting New York. They meant something to me personally, were things I wanted to do and I did them.

Multiple Streams of Determination

The rest of my dreams fall under the category of enhancement, meaning they either enhanced my life or someone else's in a variety of ways. It could be financially, emotionally, spiritually or any other way that has a positive impact.

For me, quitting my corporate sales job to launch my own magazine, creating new divisions with two Fortune 500 companies and writing my first book, *Dream Big, Win Big!*, all fit in this enhancement category. Likewise, sharing the stage with legends like Les Brown and Zig Ziglar, co-authoring a book with Olympic Gold Medalist Lanny Bassham, and launching God Encounter Television, also fit in this group.

Sometimes a dream can overlap and be both a personal dream and an enhancement dream. For me, being able to fulfill a childhood dream of performing stand-up comedy actually fits both categories because it was something I had always wanted to do, and when I did, I actually got paid to do it.

As I began to dissect my dreams and chart them from beginning to end, a pattern or cycle emerged. There were commonalities in all of them, especially the enhancement dreams. Personal dreams are tricky in the sense that, in some of them, it may not be obvious that certain things actually took place in the process. Besides, ,it's also easier to put a personal dream on hold.

For example, let's say you always wanted to visit Disney World as a child but never got to. Now that you have a family of your own, it's your dream to take them. But if you find that for some reason your plans fall through, chances are you'll find that it's not that big of a deal to say "let's wait until summer."

On the other hand, if it's your 12-year-old daughter's dream to visit Disney World and she has terminal cancer, you will do whatever it

Blueprint of a Dream

takes to make the trip. It's now an enhancement dream. Your motivation is much greater, and that's something we will take a look at later in this chapter.

As I go through the different phases of bringing a dream to life, I want you to think from the perspective of an enhancement dream. If possible, I'd like you to think of a dream you brought to life, or perhaps one that you wanted to but didn't. See if you can identify the different components and how they relate to your dream.

As I go through and describe what I will call the Dream Machine, I am going to use the example of when I quit my corporate sales job with a shoe manufacturer to launch my own niche magazine. I left a base salary and benefits to walk out on my own with no financial backing. Sound crazy? Maybe it won't after we break it down. Almost every dream of mine, including this one, at some point started with an **inspiration**. This isn't the actual dream itself but rather the catalyst or spark that got my wheels turning. More times than not it will be either some sort of pain or a cause, something that moves you.

For me, my inspiration came when I was sitting in a hotel room in Southern California during part of a 13-day sales trip. I realized at that moment how much I hated being away from my then 7-year-old son for that long. I hated missing his baseball games because I had to travel and missing his golf tournaments because I had a sales meeting. I wanted to be in control of my schedule and my time. I knew that as long as I worked for someone else that would never be the case. My wheels were turning.

The next three components can occur totally independent of each other or simultaneously. In my case, they all happened almost instantaneously. The next part of the process is the **vision**. This is the dream itself.

Multiple Streams of Determination

My dream was to launch my own business and set my own schedule and never miss another one of my son's activities.

This also ties into the next piece of the puzzle, my **motivation, or why**. Your why is what will get you going and keep you going. This may be the single biggest factor in determining whether you will see your dream through to completion. Your why has to be bigger than you, and big enough that you will not let anyone or anything come between you and your dream. Think of it this way: If your why don't make you cry, it's not big enough. We will go deeper in the importance of your why in another chapter.

After that came the **calculation** phase. This is where I started to really formulate a plan and began doing research. I wanted to not only start my own business, but try to attach it to something I loved doing and to something I knew I could do well. I knew that a perfect fit for me would be to bring golf and sales together. I loved golf and was good at sales.

After much consideration, I decided to launch a monthly junior golf magazine that would be 100 percent supported by advertising revenue. I spent several weeks doing my homework and coming up with a game plan. As things began to fall into place, I knew that this would provide the income I needed, so long as it was properly executed. I then reached the point of **realization**, the next step in the process, where I told myself, "I can do this!"

This is where we cross over from testing the waters to actually starting to believe that our dream is achieveable. This is also where our self-image kicks in. We will talk more about self-image later in the book, but keep this point fresh in your mind -- your performance will never exceed your self-image.

Blueprint of a Dream

Once I made it that far, I was rocking and rolling. But in truth,. most dreams die either directly before or after the next step. The next step in bringing your dreams to life is actually quite simple, but as I just mentioned, many people never reach this point. You must make a **decision**. That's all it is. Decide. You have to transition from *I can do this* to *I'm going to do this*.

At some point you have to make a decision that you are going to pursue your dream. But don't stop there. Follow me for a second. Three boys are sitting on a bridge overlooking a creek. Two of them decide to jump in. How many are left? If you answered one, you're wrong. The correct answer is three. You see, they only decided to jump. If half of the people who let their dreams die do so because they never decide to pursue their dream, then the other half let their dreams die because they fail to take the next step, which in reality is the most important. These people decide to act, but they never take **action**.

You can sit around all day and talk about what you are going to do and even tell everyone how you've decided to finally chase down that dream, but brother, if you never take action, it will never happen. You can quote me on that.

This one key is what prompted me to come up with my signature quote: "It's not how many dreams you have, it's how many you bring to life." My dream truly began to take shape when I handed in my letter of resignation and walked out the door. There was no turning back. I took the first step. I took action. This is where the rubber meets the road, so to speak.

I always like to remind myself that talk is cheap. And the old saying is true. A journey of a thousand miles begins with a single step. Once I quite my sales job and walked out the door, my journey had begun.

Multiple Streams of Determination

The next step is **implementation**, the period in which you begin to work your plan. For me, this is where it really got fun. I created a media kit on my iMac, made some copies and went out cold-calling, trying to sell advertising in a magazine that did not yet exist anywhere other than in my dream. To all of the entrepreneurs out there, and I'm speaking from experience, there's not a person alive who can or will sell your dream better than yourself. I feel very comfortable in saying that, if I had hired a sales team to go out and sell my dream I probably wouldn't be writing this today.

You don't have to be a salesman per se. Just share your dream with passion and people will buy into it if it makes sense. The first ad I sold was my back cover. I sold it to a national golf shaft manufacturer that told me up front that it didn't do any "local" advertising. I'm glad I decided not to listen. After making that sale I knew there was no stopping me! I was building momentum.

This led me to **continuation**, where I simply continued to implement my plan. This is also a point where you may need to evaluate and adapt if necessary. I continued to tell my story and sell advertising until I had enough money to begin printing. From the time I created my media kit to the day I had sold enough advertising to begin printing, just 29 days had elapsed. In a little less than a month, I was ready to print the first issue of my magazine. The day I went to the printer to pick up the first run of magazines is a day I'll never forget. A copy of my first issue, featuring my oldest son Caleb and PGA Tour player Sergio Garcia on the cover, hangs on my wall in a glass case to this very day. It is a daily reminder of my why and what can happen when I pursue my dreams.

That is when I reached **completion**. I had brought that dream to life. It was absolutely incredible to look back and think about that night in

Blueprint of a Dream

my hotel room in Southern California, where an idea was born, and then follow the road that led me to where I was, standing there holding a copy of my magazine. Not someone else's magazine. My magazine.

At this juncture I reached the point of **evaluation**. I had to look back on the whole process and pat myself on the back for all of the things I did right, and honestly assess areas that needed improvement. I will never dwell on an area that comes up short, but I have to acknowledge it and recognize what I can do differently next time. Even though I list evaluation as the last step and after the fact, in all reality it's something that needs to be done after each phase. I constantly evaluate and adapt when necessary. Keep in mind that it's impossible to connect the dots looking forward, but you can always connect them looking back.

When I began my quest to do my own thing, I would have never thought that the journey would lead me to some of the opportunities it has. That one magazine led to three regional editions, two in Texas and one on Florida, another magazine associated with the top regional junior golf tour in the U.S., a national junior golf radio show that I co-hosted with Valeria Ochoa from the Big Break and a junior golf television show. I've even interviewed more professional golfers and celebrities than I can name, people like Kathy Whitworth, Tom Lehman, Ivan Lendl and George Lopez, just to name a few.

My point in saying all of this is not to brag. It's merely to help you understand that even though our dreams may seem big initially, they have the potential to be much bigger than we can ever imagine. If you've ever been to a redwood forest, perhaps you'll understand. The redwoods soar to the heavens, and from the forest floor you can't even see the tree tops. But if you look on the ground, you just may find tiny cones containing even tinier seeds. The mighty redwoods all around you sprang from seeds just like that. This is the way of dreams. They hold more potential than we can fathom. But our dreams will remain just untapped potential unless we take that first step and act. That's what I did, and you can, too.

About the Author

Bobby Minoris a dynamic, passionate, speaker, author and navigator of life. Bobby's messages are Relevant, Creative and Challenging. He is a called voice for this generation as he travels across the country speaking at churches, corporations, colleges, concerts, and conferences. Bobby's theme, "Life Can Change", is evident no matter where he speaks as he is living, breathing proof that nothing and no one is beyond hope.

He is a wonderful communicator and what he teaches and speaks on comes from his heart based on his experience, not some classroom theory. Whether speaking to a group of troubled teens about overcoming adversity or to major corporations about leadership, adaptability, and making things happen, one thing is for certain, you will love his entertaining and humorous style. Bobby likes to "keep it real" so expect nothing less from him. This married, father of three is a Pastor at Waves of Faith in Fort Worth and church marketing consultant, received his ABS in Biblical Studies from Andersonville Seminary and is a life-long resident of Fort Worth, Texas. For more information please visit www.bobbyminor.com.

Chapter 10

Determination For Freedom

NAKIS THEOCHARIDES

"For things to change...YOU have to change...." That was the first thing I remember from a personal development seminar I attended two years ago. This quote is from a man I've never met, but he has been seated beside me in the car everyday for the last two years, mentoring me and teaching me life lessons. Jim Rohn is the person that changed my life tremendously. I never thought that it was possible one book or even one audio book could change your life.

I was introduced to personal development by a friend of mine. At that time I worked long hours as a Health Club manager in a 5-star hotel in Nicosia. I was enjoying my job. I was surrounded by a nice environment and interesting people, and I enjoyed challenging tasks. I had a job with prestige.

Multiple Streams of Determination

Working 12-14 hours per day, though, was not the ideal lifestyle I had in my mind, plus I wanted more income for me and my family. I started studying successful people to find out how to live the ideal life and how someone can achieve wealth. I read and listened to books and audio books, always recommended by people I respect and admire. You should always pay attention to the ones that have the results you want in the area you want. Anthony Robbins says, "If you want to be successful, find someone who has achieved the results you want, copy what they do and you'll achieve the same results." Can it be simpler than that?

The greatest philosophy I got from Jim Rohn is that it's not what happens that determines our life, it's what we do about what happens. Johnny Wimbrey says it very nicely as the YOU factor. Life has challenges, but there is one single question each individual should ask himself that will determine the quality of his life: "WHAT CAN I DO?" This is what I've said every single day for two years now. For any challenge I face, I've programmed myself to ask this question. And believe me, if you ask, you will find.

We all have our daily routines, most of the time filled with habits that we do every day. For most individuals, daily routine is the biggest trap if they want to grow and achieve something more in their lives. Jim Rohn says, "Success is nothing more than a few disciplines practiced every day," and "You cannot change your destination overnight, but you can change your direction." By changing something in your daily routine, you can achieve a different result in an amount of time.

When I used to work in gyms, I was impressed with how people were acting. Health is the most important aspect in our lives. If we don't have health, we cannot have anything. Everybody wants to have good health, and everybody knows that in order to have it, you have to take care of your body with good nutrition and regular workouts. Good health comes down to two simple factors.

But how many people are taking care of these two factors? Very few.

Why don't more do it? Because people function in their comfort zone. It's very comfortable in there and anything new creates an unpleasant feeling.

Working at the gyms I had people telling me that gyms don't work. Can you imagine that?

How come some people are healthy while others are not? Some people would say genetics. OK, genetics play a major role, but I'm not talking about genetics. I'm talking about what YOU can do. They don't want to admit they are lazy, and if they do, they are not doing something to change that. A very small percentage is willing to make the uncomfortable investment in change and make the difference.

It's often said that, in order to develop a habit, you have to continuously do the specific action for a period of 21 days. So, if you want to plant in your everyday life a habit that will bring you results, then the only thing you have to do is do this action for 21 consecutive days.

I see discipline as the power to do the uncomfortable, and by doing it I can enlarge my comfort zone and grow as a person. Operating in my comfort zone I don't grow. I am just doing what I'm already doing and having the same results over and over again. Einstein says that insanity is doing the same thing over and over again and expecting different results.

Not very long ago, I was very bad off psychologically; I had problems with my job, my relationship with my parents was not good, I broke up with my girlfriend, I was broke, and I was not in the mood to take care of my health. I was not exercising at all while before I was working out five times a week.

Multiple Streams of Determination

Have you ever heard about the domino effect, when a small change causes a similar change nearby? A series of changes in one area in my life affected other areas, negatively, of course. I was feeling weak and with no self-confidence. I wanted to get out of this situation as soon as possible.

After a lot of struggle, I figured out that I could not take care of all areas at once. A very good friend of mine opened my eyes when he suggested I focus on one area and the domino effect would work for me. I lost my belief, but I didn't lose my faith. While everything was falling apart around me, I was investing in myself, feeding my brain with personal development material every single day. Reading the books and listening to the audio material, I figured out something very logical, something we don't see when we are under certain circumstances, something that made me change my mindset and made me happy for having the difficulties. I figured out that all successful people had major difficulties during their journey for success, so I was on the right track. Until then I was focusing on my current condition and I couldn't see my potential. Struggle and difficulties give value to our successes. Without failure there is no success.

This is an excerpt from Robin Sharma's book, The Monk Who Sold his Ferrari: "Failure tests us and allows us to grow. It offers us lessons and guides us along the path of enlightenment. The teachers of the East say that every arrow that hits the bull's eye is the result of one hundred misses. It is a fundamental Law of Nature to profit through loss. Never fear failure. Failure is your friend."

I remember the day I decided to change the direction of my life. It was a Saturday morning, and I was relaxing at Phinikoudes Beach in Larnaca after a very busy week at work. I was reading Robert Kiyosaki's Rich Dad Poor Dad – Guide to Investing, in which he separates the three choices of investing:

Determination For Freedom

1. Be secure;

2. Be comfortable; and

3. Be rich.

Most people would love to be rich; however, very few people are willing to pay the price for the prize.

Kiyosaki says that if you want to achieve financial freedom, you have to make it your first choice.

If you choose to operate on the secure and comfortable zone, then you cannot achieve financial freedom. That moment I felt weird and uncomfortable. I was operating in the secure and comfortable zone, but all my life I wanted freedom. Although I was working long hours, I was in the small percentage of the people who love their jobs and I was enjoying my job. Something I could not see back then was the fact that I was leaving my life outside of the equation.

I started my entrepreneurial career part-time. I devoted 15 hours per week to my part-time activity while I was working 12-14 on my full-time job. While my colleagues were going home relaxing in front of the TV, I was working. While the "normal" people were enjoying weekends at the beaches and coffee shops, I was attending personal development seminars or reading books at my house, investing in myself. To give you an idea of my daily routine, I was leaving my house at 7 a.m. and I was going back at 11 p.m. Everybody around me thought I was crazy. My family, my friends, my colleagues, they were all telling me, "Focus on your job. Many people would love to be in your position." Still others tried to hold me back with negative thinking, telling me, "These things don't work," and "Cyprus is a small island. You won't succeed here."

I decided, however, I wanted to change, and my desire to achieve my

Multiple Streams of Determination

goal was above and beyond what other people were thinking. I programmed myself to do this daily routine for five months. It was tough, but it was a fun journey, and it was fun because I made this daily routine my comfort zone.

With the new vehicle, in four months I doubled the income I was getting from my full-time job. Even though I was in love with my job, the job was not serving the purpose of my life. It was just the wrong vehicle. During these four months I never thought about resigning from my job. However, Kiyosaki's guidelines were always in my mind. I distinctly remember a Monday morning. I was sitting in my office at work and all of a sudden I thought, "Why am I still here?" I could not find an answer. In five seconds, I decided to make a major shift in my life. Until then I was playing it safe. Being comfortable is not the right path. Freedom requires determination. Tommy Lasorda said, "The difference between the impossible and the possible lies in a person's determination."

Through this journey I learned how to discipline my disappointment. Many people, especially people that I love, tried to stop me because they thought they were "protecting" me. I admit that many times I was influenced by them, and I fell down several times. While I was down, I never stopped thinking about my goal. I imagined Jim Rohn telling me, "You will climb the mountain. They've told you it's too high, it's too far, it's too steep, it's too rocky, it's too difficult. But it's your mountain. You will climb it. I'm waiting to see you waving from the top." Investing in myself was what gave me strength to get up and continue my journey. What I realized later is that no one had the power to influence me. I was just weak and I allowed it. I found my true enemy -- myself.

The greatest value is not the results. Results are just the measure of what you become. Set any goal you want. The real value is what it will make of you as you strive to achieve the goal, the person you become. The higher the goal, the greatest person you become.

I wouldn't change the period that I had difficulties for anything. This period made me stronger and pushed me to my limits. Life is full of challenges. This is unavoidable. So you can either be sad for the rest of your life for what happened, or do something and use the challenge as an opportunity to learn more for the future. If you survived from the first wave, you know how to handle the second.

I am a firm believer that everything happens for a reason. We might not be able to see the reason at that specific time, but this will come up soon. When a door closes, a window opens.

Define your goal, put together a plan to achieve it, and take massive action on a daily basis to make this goal a reality.

My favorite movie character, Rocky Balboa, said to his son: "The world ain't all sunshine and rainbows. It's a very mean and nasty place and I don't care how tough you are, it will beat you to your knees and keep you there permanently if you let it. You, me, or nobody is going to hit as hard as life. But it ain't about how hard you hit; it's about how hard you can get hit, and keep moving forward, how much you can take, and keep moving forward. That's how winning is done. Now, if you know what you're worth, go out and get what you're worth, but you gotta be willing to take the hits, and not pointing fingers saying you ain't where you are because of him, or her, or anybody. Cowards do that and that ain't you. You're better than that!"

"WHAT CAN I DO?" Ask this question everyday for anything that happens. Take the responsibility to take action and be among the few who go for their dreams, because if YOU don't, no one will.

What happened before belongs to the past. It doesn't determine your future. You are standing right here right now facing the present and the future. What are you going to do about it? WHAT CAN YOU DO?

About the Author

Nakis Theocharides is from Cyprus, a Greek island on the Eastern part of the Mediterranean. He holds a Bachelor of Arts Degree in Business Administration with a Marketing Concentration from the University of LaVerne, Athens Campus. He is also an Aerobic and Fitness Instructor, graduating from GR.A.F.T.S. in Athens and from UK Central YMCA Qualifications, a specialized body for health and fitness in the UK. He has worked in many gyms and health clubs and he has presented in various fitness conventions and seminars in Greece and Cyprus.

From September 2006 and for three and one half years, he was working as Health Club Manager at Hilton Cyprus, the most historical hotel of Nicosia, capital of Cyprus.

Now working as an entrepreneur, he has a major purpose in his life -- to help as many people as possible improve their lives and achieve their dreams. He owns an international business with customers and partners in different countries, traveling and inspiring people for greatness.

You can reach Nakis Theocharides at:

Website: www.nakisaero.com

Email: nakisaero@gmail.com

Facebook: www.facebook.com/nakis.theocharides

Chapter 11

Don't Believe the Hype!

TERRY MCGEE

Growing up as a child in the inner city, I did not have a whole lot of positive influences in my life.

I saw very early on that success was about graduating from high school at a minimum and going on to college. After that, the next step was to find gainful employment.

Now, the funny part is that, from here, you just work 40-plus hours a week for 40-plus years, and if everything goes OK and you get a couple of breaks, you can retire and have a couple thousand dollars a month retirement pay.

The only other option, I was told as a young fella, was to be tall or big and play basketball or football. Well, I was neither, so off to work I went.

Multiple Streams of Determination

After punching a time clock for a couple of years, I began to understand that this was not for me. But I did nothing about it. Fast forward 25 years, and I started seeing the light. If "I" wanted to do something about it, "I" had to do something about it.

You see, to make a change, two things have to happen: You have to decide that you really want it and YOU have to make it happen. I truly believe that GOD gave every person a gift. It may be talent in singing, great athleticism, a gift to preach, a gift to teach and so on. I also believe he wants us to be successful at whatever we do.

But here is what happens. As young children, we start believing the hype! But it is within each and every one of us to break free of this thinking and achieve success. Success is whatever YOU determine it is. For some, that 40/40 thing is success; for most of us, it is just called life. But I am here to tell you that you have a choice.

You see, a choice is a GOD-given ability. We make good choices and we make bad ones. We make some that will define our character. I have chosen to not to believe the hype. I have chosen to do it my way (thanks, Frank Sinatra). I will not be stopped! I will build a legacy for my children and grandchildren. I will take everyone on this ride who wants something else.

Choose your goals and go for it. Never let someone tell you that what you want is impossible. I just watched a python eat an alligator on the National Geographic TV channel. Now, what would have happened if the python told his buddy that he was going to eat a gator? The conversation probably would have gone like this: (First python) Dude, that gator been messing with me all day. I think I am going to eat it. (Other python) Dude!! Are you crazy!? That thing is like five times bigger than you! You can't win. (First python) Yeah, you are probably right. I think that I am going to just keep running from it.

Don't Believe the Hype!

But this particular python did not "believe the hype." And these are the kinds of obstacles we always face as well. You may want more but the people you are running with may not want more. Some will hate you just because you have the nerve to dream big! So their job is to rob you of your dream (or as we say, haters). "Marvel not, my brethren, if the world hate you." 1 John 4-13. You see, even the Bible speaks of haters. Follow your dreams despite what someone else may think. Be encouraged to pursue YOUR life happiness regardless of the criticism you will endure. Remember, this is your dream. You will have to fight for your dreams. Nothing will just be given to you. Remember, anything worth having is worth fighting for. Nothing worthwhile will come easy.

Even as a ward of corporate America, I was different. I was not ordinary. You see, I don't do ordinary. And I saw myself doing ordinary things and going ordinary places. Now don't be confused. I am not saying I am better than anyone. I am saying no one is better than me. If they can go shop there, then I want to go shop there. If they can buy a car "there" I want to buy a car "there." "There" is my "there," and your "there" may be different. But all I am telling you is, you can make it happen on your own terms if you have a will to win.

Great things can take place in the blink of an eye if you are prepared. You see, when opportunity meets preparation, good things happen (some people call this luck). Luck is actually when someone wins the lottery. They are banking on a certain amount of numbers to match the piece of paper in their hands. Think about it. Only one winning number and millions of players; the system wins again. When you prepare for success and the opportunity comes, everyone will always win. Advantage, the people.

Don't let the person in the mirror discourage or stop you from realizing

Multiple Streams of Determination

your full potential. That person can be detrimental to your dreams or be the driving force behind it. Tell yourself every day, "I will succeed no matter what!" If you do this, you will slowly start transforming into the person you were meant to be. I am not telling you what I heard; I am telling you what I know. I myself am still transforming. I started taking matters into my own hands. I represent the common man. Nothing special, but I have started looking at it like this: Bill Gates and Donald Trump were born just like me, they put their pants on just like me, they have 24 hours in a day, just like me, so I wondered, "Why them?" Then it hit me! They not only dreamed (yes, like me) they actually went out and made it happen! There are countless others as well, but the difference is still the same. They made it happen. One percent of the United States of America has more wealth than the combined total of the bottom ninety percent. All that means is that one percent decided to do something in their life to make dreams come true. They refused to accept that 40/40 thing I was telling you about earlier. Some still do it, but it is by "choice" now (there is that word again).

We have the power within to change a negative circumstance into a positive one. OK, so you are working in corporate America now, but you want out. Start talking to that person in the mirror and let him or her know as well. Find what you are passionate about and work on it every chance you get. Replace your three hours of watching TV with working on your dream. Trade in the two hours a day on the phone with aspiring to make it happen. Take the time to reach as high as you can, to make it happen for you. Don't believe the hype!

I never did anything spectacular in school. I did just enough to graduate. I remember waiting impatiently until the very last hour to see if I had achieved the first major part of life (graduating). Now this did not happen because I was dumb or slow. I just made a lot of bad decisions, like skipping class to go to the mall, not doing homework and getting

Don't Believe the Hype!

kicked out a couple of times. And when I did attend class, I was the ultimate class clown and interrupted class frequently. I had no idea of the struggles of life that would soon become apparent to me. Now as I look back, WOW!

And yet here I am now changing my destiny. I will not let my start dictate my finish! So no matter where you are in life, you can still have a say in your destiny. God is very forgiving; don't let past transgressions hold you back. If the creator can forgive, so can the person in the mirror! Your past is just that, the past. The future holds so much more for you if you want it. You cannot achieve what you don't believe. Also don't let the "cool" factor get you down, either. Don't get held back by such thoughts as, "I am too cool to let my partners see me in this way." You will have to change your friends, or "change" your friends. Keep in mind, this is for you. And it is between you and the creator.

You see, I am trainable and coachable (and I have great teachers), and when you can reduce the "me" factor in yourself to let others help you, you now become "unstoppable" (thanks for that one, Johnny). What was once a very average and bleak future now shines brighter than the sun. Well, maybe not the sun, because that was created by God! But very bright. Again, there is nothing special about me. I just refuse to lose. At this point, it is no longer even an option. I just get it now. Someone dangled that carrot in my face a bit too long! I have it now and have tasted the fruits of my dreams. All systems full steam ahead! Disconnect the brake!

The most rewarding part of this is the people. I love watching people succeed. I love talking to them, I love visiting them. Being around these people is intoxicating. It makes me want to do better. To all the professional baseball players that I know to the book authors that I know and to that very successful businessman man that I know, thanks

Multiple Streams of Determination

for letting me taste what hard work and determination can do. I cannot wait to help others achieve what they thought was impossible. I have seen it and now I'm stretching for it myself. Instead of taking that two-to-four week vacation every year, how about working two-to-four weeks a year and vacation the rest? Let's do this together.

I now believe it is in each and every one of us to go beyond average. When I talk to my family and friends now, I tell them how much control they have over themselves and urge them not to be limited by what they have been conditioned to believe (the hype). We see all these big stars like Beyonce and others and think, "Hmm, I could have done that." Well, you can. But just be prepared to work for what you want. I suggest reading up on your favorite stars and see just what it takes to reach the pinnacle. I will bet that you will not see much difference between you and them other than the work that is necessary to get there. No one gets there without sacrifice and hard work. Sorry, but I have got to give you the bad as well as the good. The thing is that the bad gets better and the good becomes outstanding! A sacrifice lasts but a moment, but the results can be everlasting!

This whole thing is about mindset. If I said I have a magic seed I'll sell for $1,000, and if you plant it and cultivate it for two years you will reap $1 million as the harvest, I will have hundreds if not thousands breaking my door down to get this seed. But here is a little secret between you and me. The seed is actually free and you already have it! Tah da! How is that for a magic trick? We are led to believe that you have to work until you are a senior citizen to get the harvest. This harvest is yours and mine at whatever time in life we want it.

In closing, I just want to say that you shouldn't convince yourself that you cannot win at the highest of levels! Don't believe the hype, and dream big! Let's get there together.

Terry McGee

About the Author

Terry McGee was born and raised in Rockford, Illinois. He graduated from Thomas Jefferson High School in 1981, and then went on to attend Devry Institute of Technology pursuing a two-year diploma in electronics.

He worked at various jobs and held multiple duties in the corporate world for approximately 27 years, spending the last 12 in the mail industry. He started as an electronic tech and worked through the ranks to obtain a management position in customer service. McGee received many accolades from customers because of a positive attitude in times of adversity.

McGee also owned and operated McGee Networks Plus, a small company that specialized in the sales and service of electronic equipment.

McGee was introduced to network marketing in January 2010. This proved to be a perfect match for his goal of attaining financial success and his desire to help others. McGee believes network marketing is the best personal improvement method around. He is now building a team and using the techniques learned to help others realize their dreams and reach their full potential.

McGee now resides in Little Elm, Texas, with his wife, eldest daughter and son. He also has two daughters attending the University of Houston in Houston, Texas.

Multiple Streams of Determination

McGee is a WorldVentures independent rep. For more information on WorldVentures, see mnp.worldventures.biz.

Email: mcgeeterrye@yahoo.com

Twitter: http://twitter.com/ TEMcGeeSr

Chapter 12

Changing to a New You
So the "Real" You Can Shine Through

BY LES BROWN

Sometimes it's not about changing to become the person you *want* to be; it's about changing to become the person you *need* to be. There is a whole big, expectant world out there waiting on you to do the things you were destined to do – and the only obstacle in the way is YOU. Personal growth can help you conquer that obstacle, but you must first be a willing participant.

Once you have decided that you are that willing participant, follow these four easy stages of increased awareness to help you begin this journey to a "new you." Let's take a quick look at how 1) self-knowledge, 2) self-approval, 3) self-commitment and 4) self-fulfillment intertwine to help you consciously step into greatness.

Multiple Streams of Inspiration

First of all, in order to see yourself beyond your current circumstances, you must master **self-knowledge**. Simply ask yourself, "What drives me?" And then pause long enough to hear your response. Try to understand what outside forces – positive or negative – are influencing your answer. Many of us suffer from what I call "unconscious incompetence." That means we don't know that we don't know, which leaves the door wide open for others to tell us what we think we need to know. Therefore, before you can fully wake up and change your life, you must understand the frame of reference from which you view the world. Study yourself, study the forces behind your personal history, and study the people in your life. This will help liberate you to grow beyond your imagination.

The second, and perhaps most crucial, stage of personal growth is **self-approval**. Once you begin to know and understand yourself more completely, then you must accept and love yourself. Self-hatred, self-loathing, guilt and long-standing anger only work to block your growth. Don't direct your energy toward this type of self-destruction. Instead, practice self-love and forgiveness and watch how they carry over into your relationships, your work and the world around you, opening up the possibility for others to love you, too. If you need help in boosting your self-approval, try these steps: 1) focus on your gifts, 2) write down at least five things you like about yourself, 3) think about the people who make you feel special, and 4) recall your moments of triumph.

When you are committed to taking life on, life opens up for you. Only then do you become aware of things that you were not aware of before. That is the essence of **self-commitment**. It's like the expanded consciousness that comes whenever I commit to a diet. Suddenly, everywhere I turn, there is FOOD! Or how about when you buy a new car? Suddenly you notice cars exactly like yours, everywhere you go. Well, likewise, when you make a commitment – when your life awareness is expanded – opportunities previously unseen begin to appear, bringing you to a higher level. In this posture, you are running your life, rather than running *from* life.

The fourth stage of self awareness is **self-fulfillment**. Once you have committed to something and achieved it, you then experience a sense of success and empowerment, otherwise known as fulfillment. Your drive for self-fulfillment should be an unending quest; a continual sequence of testing self-knowledge, fortifying self-approval, renewing self-commitment and striving for new levels of self-fulfillment. Once you have accomplished a goal and reached a level of self-fulfillment, it is then time to go back to the first stage in the cycle.

These four stages create synergy for a conscious awareness of your personal growth. But what about learning to deal with all this from a subconscious standpoint? A very interesting book I read recently entitled, "A Whole New Mind," by Daniel H. Pink, explains that the key to success today is in the hands of the individual with a whole different kind of thinking than what our informational age has molded us to. The metaphorically "left brain" capacities that fueled that Information Era, are no longer sufficient. Instead, ""right brain" traits of inventiveness, empathy, joyfulness and meaning – increasingly will determine who flourishes and who flounders." (Pink, 2007)

I highly recommend that, in the midst of your busy schedule, you pick up this book and engage yourself to a fresh look at what it takes to excel. As I mentioned before, the only real obstacle in your path to personal growth and a fulfilling life is you. If everything around you is changing and growing – then change and grow. Do it today. Remember, we are all counting on you to step into your greatness!

Now even after making all of these changes what would you say if someone walked up to you and asked, "Who are you?" Would you stutter or

Multiple Streams of Inspiration

hesitate before giving some sort of answer? Would you make up something that sounded impressive, but that you know isn't exactly true? Well, to accurately answer the question of who you are, you must first get in touch with the person who lives and breathes on the inside of you.

When you know and understand who you were made to be, you can begin to tap into the innate power of your own uniqueness. That power allows you the freedom to no longer let life hold you back because of nonsense based on what you've done or not done. It gives you the positive energy to move forward in spite of those things.

You are a unique individual. Think about it, out of 400,000,000 sperm, one was spared to allow you to be here today. Then once you got here, you came with total exclusivity! I know for a fact, as a twin myself, how you can look like someone else, even sound like that person, yet when you consider the total you, there is only one. Wow! Just let that thought sink down in you for a moment.

Now, hopefully that helps you to realize that there is a certain quality on the inside of you that was given to you – and only you – in order to make a difference in this world. Whatever that quality is, it was not intended for you to sit on it, or waste it away. Oh no, it was given to you for a purpose! You cannot, however, learn what that purpose is unless you look inside and see what makes your existence so special.

Don't waste time trying to find "you" in other people. When you compare yourself to others, or try to be like them, you deny yourself – and the universe – the opportunity to be blessed by the gifts and talents that were given only to you. You are destined to achieve great things in *your* own special way; not in the same manner as your friends, relatives, co-workers, colleagues or even mentors. Doing so will only leave you unsatisfied. When you are not satisfied, regret creeps in.

Changing to a New You . . .

If you don't know this already, let me share a little secret with you: In order to live a good life – a life full of purpose and resolve – you must live it with NO REGRETS!

Most people go through their whole life with a long "would've, could've, should've" list. The truth of the matter is, once you've lived through a day, an hour, or a minute, it's done. You cannot go back. So get over it! Go forward! There's so much more for you to accomplish that you don't have time to live in the past trying to fix things.

Keep in mind, though, that living in the past and reflecting on the past are two totally different things. You *can* look back – and you should – in order to determine what it was about certain experiences that brought you joy and satisfaction, or grief and despair; what caused you to grow and expand your horizons, or left you stagnant and short-sighted.

Although you cannot relive the past, you can learn much about yourself as a result of having lived it. That requires a lot of honesty with yourself, as well as a willingness to do whatever it takes to reach your destiny. Of all the things you can acquire in this life, the most valuable has to be the knowledge of what role you are to play on this earth, for the sake of your destiny.

My favorite book says to *"Lean not on your own understanding, but in all your ways, acknowledge Him and He will direct your paths."* In other words, don't rely solely on your own insight regarding what your role is. There's a Creator who made you and knows you better than you know yourself. Therefore, in everything you do, in every direction you take, recognize and consult with that Creator. That's what it means to look on the inside – not at others.

Now, you will have a real answer when someone asks, "Who are you?" You can assure them that, without a shadow of a doubt, you are not

Multiple Streams of Inspiration

here by accident. You can articulate with unwavering conviction what it is you were put on this earth to do. **Learn to do this and watch the real "you" shine through!**

World renowned motivational speaker, Les Brown, is also a best selling author. He has several more books soon to join the ranks of "Live Your Dreams," "It's Not Over Until You Win" and "Up Thoughts for Down Times." Les hosts a weekly radio show, "On Fire to Inspire," on Philadelphia's inspiration station, Praise 103.9. Catch the show live each Sunday, 7pm – 9pm EST via the Internet at www.Praise1039.com. To view Les' upcoming events, or to book him as your next keynote speaker, visit www.lesbrown.com.

About the Author

Les Brown is a top Motivational Speaker, Speech Coach, and Best-Selling Author, loving father and grandfather, whose passion is empowering youth and helping them have a larger vision for their lives.

Les Brown's straight-from-the-heart, high-energy, passionate message motivates and engages all audiences to step into their greatness, providing them with the motivation to take the next step toward living their dream. Les Brown's charisma, warmth and sense of humor have impacted many lives.

Les Brown's life itself is a true testament to the power of positive thinking and the infinite human potential. Leslie C. Brown was born on February 17, 1945, in an abandoned building on a floor in Liberty City, a low-income section of Miami, Florida, and adopted at six weeks of age by Mrs. Mamie Brown, a 38 year old single woman, cafeteria cook and domestic worker, who had very little education or financial means, but a very big heart and the desire to care for Les Brown and his

Changing to a New You . . .

twin brother, Wesley Brown. Les Brown calls himself "Mrs. Mamie Brown's Baby Boy" and claims "All that I am and all that I ever hoped to be, I owe to my mother".

Les Brown's determination and persistence searching for ways to help Mamie Brown overcome poverty and his philosophy "do whatever it takes to achieve success" led him to become a distinguished authority on harnessing human potential and success. Les Brown's passion to learn and his hunger to realize greatness in himself and others helped him to achieve greatness in spite of not having formal education or training beyond high school.

"My mission is to get a message out that will help people become uncomfortable with their mediocrity. A lot of people are content with their discontent. I want to be the catalyst that enables them to see themselves having more and achieving more."

Les moved to Detroit and rented an office with an attorney, where he slept on the floor and welcomed his reality stating that he did not even want a blanket or pallet on the cold, hard floor to keep him motivated to strive. In 1986, Les entered the public speaking arena on a full-time basis and formed his own company, Les Brown Enterprises, Inc..

Les Brown rose from a hip-talking morning DJ to broadcast manager; from community activist to community leader; from political commentator to three-term State legislator in Ohio; and from a banquet and nightclub emcee to premier Keynote Speaker for audiences as big as 80,000 people, including Fortune 500 companies and organizations all over the world.

As a caring and dedicated Speech Coach, Les Brown has coached and trained numerous successful young speakers all over the nation.

Multiple Streams of Inspiration

Les Brown is also the author of the highly acclaimed and successful books, "Live Your Dreams" and "It's Not Over Until You Win", and former host of The Les Brown Show, a nationally syndicated daily television talk show which focused on solutions and not on problems.

For more information please visit www.lesbrown.com.

Chapter 13

Choose To Win Now

DAVID IMONITIE, JR

I believe there is a force and science that allows all men and women to accomplish great things in their lives. I have been very fortunate to use this factor and power to overcome great challenges in my own life. This powerful force that has driven me toward success all started with a choice -- a decision to win and to WIN NOW!

CHOOSE TO WIN NOW has been a dominating thought in my life that has led me down a path of ultimate fulfillment and success. My goal and sole purpose for writing this book is to share with you how you, too, can CHOOSE TO WIN NOW and accomplish phenomenal results in every area of your life, specifically in the area of business and finance.

Multiple Streams of Determination

CHOOSE TO WIN NOW is a belief system that has been developed over many years of study and practical use in my life. It has created incredible life changing results on a global scale, even to the degree of building a multi-million-dollar-a-month enterprise in the industry of network marketing in less than two years.

I also have been blessed with the privilege of teaching and training thousands of people all over the world on how to believe, and more importantly, on how to grow their capacity to believe.

To help you understand this system in its entirety, I will walk you through practical steps and formulas that you can utilize right away to realize every DVD (Desire Vision Dream) for your life.

One of the first things that I did was learn how to raise the bar in my life. Raising the bar is a philosophy I learned from my personal mentors, Mr. Holton and Mrs. Buggs. Using this philosophy, over the course of a few years, has impacted me dramatically. After dropping out of college and being driven toward starting my first company at the age of 21, I had very little belief and was unaware of the action steps to take. However, I did know what results I was looking for.

Starting out with blind faith and learning the action steps I needed to take, I knew the results would come. The question I had was, "How do I go about raising my belief?" This was the main factor to my success. I had to learn how to raise my belief. I believe in order to understand how to do something, you first have to understand what it is.

Belief is a state of mind. Belief is muscle that must be exercised every day. Belief is an idea that must be accepted as truth. So in order to raise my belief, I had to raise the amount of ideas that I planted in my mind. Belief is also a conviction that is at the root of every human being. Everything that you accomplish in life will always be based on your level of belief. To believe in anything is to own it. I looked up the meaning of the word BELIEVE, and what I found was the definition, "loved by the gods." That makes sense. As the carpenter from Galilee said, "If thou canst believe, all things are possible to him that believeth."

RAISING THE BAR

In raising the bar, your belief must be at a certain level, and consequently, your actions will follow suit. This begins with you choosing to elevate the standards for your life. What you believe will ultimately determine how high you rise. If you were to believe you had a billion dollars, you would have to raise your level of belief and see yourself with a billion dollars. After this process, action would be the next step to take. Action is persistently doing a certain amount of activity over a consistent period of time, while developing the necessary skills required to achieve exactly what you believe for yourself.

THERE ARE FOUR KEYS TO RAISING THE BAR

Key Number One The first key is to design a picture of your life that you simply cannot live without. Ask yourself what the dominating picture is in your mind. Holton Buggs, in the CASH COW AUDIO SERIES, says, "You don't get what you want in life. You only get what you picture." Most people want incredible success, wealth, the freedom to travel, etc., but they never take the time to picture it. Therefore, they never take the action steps to obtain what they want. Every single day, you must place in your mind a picture of success. Designing what your life looks like and putting it down on paper is vital to raising the bar in your life. By implementing three steps in your daily life, you can attain anything you desire. First, you must design and build your life in your mind. Second, you must solidify your design by writing it

Multiple Streams of Determination

down on paper. Third, you have to undertake massive action to physically build your desired life. These three steps will assist you in turning your dreams into a much-welcomed reality.

Key Number Two The second key to raising the bar is to determine what inner conflicts must be resolved in your life to accomplish your goals. This is where the rubber meets the road. One cannot say, "I want to be wealthy, rich, powerful, etc.," and watch TV all day long. Something would have to be removed from your life to make room for something greater to move in. You will be orchestrating a decision to make a short-term sacrifice for a long-term gain. This decision must be determined with no turning back, and you must burn the ship of retreat. Napoleon Hill in *Think and Grow Rich* said, "There is no such thing as something for nothing." This is something you must decide immediately. When you hear the word decide, it rhymes with some other words... homicide and suicide. What is the common nature of these words? Something dies. When you CHOOSE TO WIN NOW, all other options to fail die!

Key Number Three The third key is to find a mentor. Remember, we are still talking about raising the bar. A mentor is the only exit from your past. You can either learn from your personal experience or learn from the experience of another. A mentor is the greatest gift anyone can have. The mentor must choose you and you must choose the mentor. A mentor is a champion who believes in you, but more importantly, you believe in him or her. Every person who has ever raised the bar in his or her life or won in any undertaking has had the great gift of a mentor. Your mentor will give you a living and breathing picture of success. **WARNING:** When you find a mentor, **DO NOT TAKE HIM OR HER FOR GRANTED!** When I found my mentor, I had a thousand dollars to my name. With the guidance of my incredible mentor, I became a millionaire in less than two years. I made it my focus to learn from his experience and allow his mentorship to lead me to phenomenal success.

Key Number Four Creating a plan and taking action is the fourth and final key to raising the bar in your life. Once you've put your plan of action on paper, you must continually execute the first three keys and continue to work your plan until it becomes your reality. Until you see the desired results, your actions must consistently continue. In creating this plan, you must have the right tools, strategies, and skills. These will come based on how well you execute your first three keys in raising the bar and increasing the standards for your life.

Because CHOOSE TO WIN NOW is a belief system, I want to share with you some specific ways of growing belief. I call these the "3V's" to live by. Your capacity to believe is based on how consistent you are with these three components. You have been blessed with a conscious mind that allows you to accomplish goals with an attentive focus. Also, you have been blessed with a subconscious mind. Remember when you first started driving? You had two hands on the wheel, you were determined, and there was no talking or disturbances. You were focused. After a period of consistent driving action and repetition, your subconscious mind kicked in, and you now don't really have to think about how to drive. This is your auto-pilot, the super-human inside of you that can accomplish all things, with little to no help from your conscious mind.

THREE VALUABLE COMPONENTS TO GROWING YOUR CAPACITY TO BELIEVE

Verbalization is the first component to growing your belief. The simple definition of the word verbalization is "the expression of words with passion and emotion." The words that you speak come from the inside of a living and breathing object. We have all learned that death and

Multiple Streams of Determination

life is in the power of the tongue. However, I do not think anyone has ever explained why this is true. I believe this statement to be true because we are alive. Verbalization gives you the ability to send clear and precise instructions to your subconscious mind. It allows you to speak life into what it is you believe. This is a practice you must live by.

What I have also learned is that each human being believes in himself more than in any other person, so what you say to you is the absolute truth. This is why communication to one's self is the greatest skill you must learn. Other words for verbalization include affirmation and incantation. It does not matter what you call it. What matters is that it is utilized consistently with passion, emotion, and intensity. The power of words is incalculable. After all, the world was created through the spoken word.

Seventy to eighty percent of your life will be guided by the thoughts and the words that you speak. Mom said it best: "Garbage in, garbage out." So the words that you put inside of you must be words that are congruent with winning. This is a seven day a week activity. You must not fall off the path that leads to life. Make sure the words you speak give life.

The second component is **Visualization**. Visualization is the process of holding on to mental images for a consistent period of time. Images you see on a regular basis become part of your life. I call this "setting up success parameters." A part of setting up success parameters is placing pictures of what you want to come to pass all around you. Most people believe in a dream or vision board, but I believe in a dream environment. Every part of your environment -- your home, your car, your office, everywhere -- should include a prominent picture of your future.

For visualization to work, you must have references. For you to have a mental picture, you must first have a physical picture. Visualization is a powerful force that takes you toward your future. You can have everything that you want using visualization. Get pictures of where you want to go, where you want to live, what you want to drive, the kind of family environment you desire, etc. Any and everything that you would ever desire is yours with the power of visualization. Even when you close your eyes, you can still see the future. The future is always brighter and more compelling than your present situation.

Knowing that your present situation is a result of your previous thoughts, using visualization will give you new thoughts to create a future filled with pictures that are all around you. Give yourself the gift of a **Vivid Experience** of what you are verbalizing and visualizing for your life. This is the most important step. A vivid experience is the visualization booster. I have seen in my life that a vivid experience has the most potent and dynamic impact on how a person believes.

A vivid experience is placing yourself in the environment of the vision that impregnates your mind with your future. What you have experienced in your life, you believe. If you believe you will have a million dollars, find a way to associate with a millionaire. If you believe you will own a dream car or a dream home, go test drive the car, and walk through the home. An experience is a trail; it is a test. An experience is your past. When you give yourself a vivid experience of what you visualize, you are creating and attaching the emotions inside of you that will cause you to believe in a completely elevated capacity. This vivid experience gives you the emotions of how it feels to have what you want, before you have it.

Most people only experience the past failures of their lives without giving themselves the experience of their desired future. You only believe what has happened in your life, so use a vivid experience of what you want to create a new reality. It is vital to understand that at all times in

Multiple Streams of Determination

your life, the choices and decisions you make effect the seasons you will be in tomorrow. When you decide to win and make a difference in your life, challenges will appear right away. Stay focused on the end result. Begin with the end in mind.

I made a decision to win now when I was living with my dad on a twin-size bed and driving an old beat-up Malibu I called the Blue Booboo. During that tough time, with no money, no future, I was always grateful that my parents, David and Kunbi Imonitie, instilled in me great values and the tenacity to win. Think and Win Big, along with several other audios, *The Strangest Secret*, *Think and Grow Rich*, and *Building Your Network Marketing Business*, were audios I listened to everyday to reprogram my mind for success. I heard on one of the audios that WIN meant you had to be Willing, take Initiative, and Never ever, ever, ever quit. With this formula, I created one of my own for my life, and I want to give it to you. It is what I call the success formula: Desire + Skills x Faith = Success.

You must have a burning Desire. Then you must have the patience to develop the skills necessary, and then have the Faith that will accelerate you to another level in your life. This formula has been used for thousands of years by great achievers. You have heard that faith without works is dead, so put the work behind your faith. Faith comes from hearing and hearing the word. This is the first proven method to grow your faith and belief.

Finally, I want to give you the greatest gift of all -- knowing that you've already won. You are just showing the world how you did it. CHOOSE TO WIN NOW.

About the Author

A college drop out, David started with his first network marketing company at the age of 21. By the age of 27 he has reached the very top of the network marketing industry and is among the top 5 income earners in the fastest growing network marketing company today.

David credits his success, after years of failing in the industry, to the incredible mentorship and coaching of Mr. Holton and Earlene Buggs. From this dynamic couple he has learned several principles that govern how to create wealth. Today David has taken these principles along with several wealth building philosophies and is now coaching and mentoring thousands of individuals to lead the revolution for financial freedom.

Mentor. Coach. Leader. These words have been used to describe David Imonitie, but, as a "Do It First" leader, David has focused on one major philosophy; help people get what they want out of life and in return you will have everything you want out of life.

Over the years, David has helped and shown people all over the world to dream big and more importantly that those dreams will become a reality with hard work and determination, but above all learning the principle that YOU BECOME WHAT YOU THINK ABOUT.

Having a definiteness of purpose is the most important tool one must have to accomplish dreams and goals. David's skills and coaching strategies have been proven to help several individuals to obtain a six figure income, and that's just the beginning of David's definite of purpose to produce one thousand six-figure income earners by way of the industry of network marketing before the age of thirty.

For more information please visit www.davidimonitie.com.

Chapter 14

I Am In Love With My Life

GEORGINA DRUCE

I was born with a silver spoon in my mouth.

I had always been very lucky. Well, that's how I saw my life. I had lots of freedom. I used to ride my pony, Topsy, into Lechlade, our local village, and tie her up to one of the trees while I went shopping. I would go riding to see local friends for lunch, and have driving lessons up the drive -- all sorts of magical things!

I knew most of the shop keepers and I felt very blessed. I went to the local school, a convent, also in the village, run by very kind and well-meaning nuns. I had lots of friends and I was into everything, especially all forms of sport. We lived on a beautiful little farm; we had so many animals we did not have names for them all. Life seemed very easy, joyful, and simple. I was very loved and I had a lot of love to give.

Multiple Streams of Determination

And then, in 1980, my amazing father took himself out of the house, into the stable, and shot himself. I was in shock. We were all in shock. My darling mother found him slumped in the stable and the story she fed us was "how peaceful he looked."

Killing yourself was not something I had ever imagined someone could possibly want to do to themselves. Daddy was diabetic, very overweight, he drank a lot, smoked like crazy, and was in debt, big debt. Mummy had been with another man, and Daddy had been told by the doctor that if he went on eating, drinking and smoking like he was, then he could expect to lose his eyesight and lose his legs within 18 months. So life for Daddy had reached such a place of desperation in so many areas that he thought "we would all be better off without him." I think he wrote this in a note, although I never saw one.

We sold the house, the farm, and all the animals and moved to my Godfather's bungalow. Then along came Peter, my very lovely stepfather, who took my mother under his wing. They were married within a year. This caused a little trouble locally because their friends thought it was all too quick. For me it was brilliant as I had seen how miserable my mother was and I thanked God she now had Peter with her. She looked really happy about her decision and her new life. We moved to a really beautiful house in Chalford Hill.

Then six years later tragedy stuck again. Two policemen turned up at the house. My mother's face fell when she saw them. I had no idea what it could mean. Will, my wonderful brother, and I were asked to stay in the sitting room to watch TV, a documentary on whales. Mummy came into the sitting room in floods of tears. My elder brother, Martin, had hanged himself in Epping Forest. He had got into drugs while at Harrow and had continued to use them after he left, and over time drug use had scrambled his head so much he could not see a way out. He had been married for a while but was divorced when he died, leaving a beautiful single mother, Regine, and a beautiful daughter, Zaza.

So there I was, loving my life and then, in 1980 and 1986, tragedy struck twice. I felt very confused and so I put my attention into working and doing the best I could, grabbing opportunities and going for life. I married my wonderful first husband, Charlie, in 1986. This marriage lasted only seven years before we divorced. I have not seen him for many years now. I am, though, very grateful to him for all the amazing lessons I learnt while being married to him. He is a very beautiful and wonderful soul.

I am also so grateful to both my darling Daddy and my wonderful brother Martin for the gifts they have given me. Wow, did they wake me up and shake me up, and as a result I started to question everything.

So I started to search for answers to all my questions. I went to psychics, joined the College of Psychic Studies, went on courses and immersed myself in many areas of personal growth. I remember having tears of joy when I really got that a soul lives on no matter what happens in the present life. I felt so joyful knowing about reincarnation, and what a blessing it is.

My journey continued. I kept asking questions, going on courses, meeting amazing people, and learning and opening up to all sorts of things I had not known about before. I love the expression, "You don't know what you don't know until you know what you don't know." There is so much out there for us to tap into if we are willing to ask outstanding questions and go searching.

I then married my darling soulmate, Michael, a very beautiful and magical soul. Then tragedy struck a third time. Our first baby died

Multiple Streams of Determination

in my womb at 24 weeks. We called him Felix and I gave birth to our still-born son. He was put to sleep in my stomach before he was born, because the fluid around him had leaked out and my body was squashing his. We gave him a funeral, which just Michael and I attended. It felt so much easier to keep it small, simple and beautiful.

Then we had our two amazing sons, Ollie and Henry. They bring us endless joy and endless fun. We are deeply blessed and so proud, as you can imagine.

In the middle of all these challenges, I kept having to find ways to really be in love with my life again. I found that by doing certain things I could create a life that I was in love with no matter what was going on around me. I started to focus only on the things that made me feel good. I now move my body to get oxygen into me and to shift my energy field so I feel good. I listen to music I love, I talk to people I love. Sharing ourselves with others is always so magical for both parties, giving time to listen, really listen to each other. I look at beautiful pictures, and watch funny movies. And I meditate. Meditation is not an option. It's a must! It's me time to check in with my divine peacefulness and with God. I light a candle and look at the flame, I take time to smell the roses. And I celebrate.

I choose to have an amazing life, a life that I love, and I keep my focus on feeling great and doing all the things I love. I choose to think that everything I am doing is amazing and that I am being a fantastic wife, mother, and friend. I choose to turn events into positives, always finding something to be grateful for in everything. This way it feels good and when I feel good life is good.

I am a survivor! Nothing stops me from how I choose to feel. I have rediscovered how to be in love with my life, in love with me, and deeply grateful, always finding a way to succeed in everything, feeling grate-

I Am In Love With My Life

ful and feeling abundance in every area of my life, no matter what the current circumstances look like!

That amazing feeling of being in love is such a gift -- whether you are in love with a man, a friend, an animal, a tree, a flower, the moon, the water, whatever. Keep that feeling and grow it and grow it and grow it until it becomes an everyday loving feeling you can tap into easily. Build the love muscle. Regard it like muscle you need to train up until it's really strong, and then keep it that way. It's a bit like going to the gym. You find a weakness and you work at it to grow it and then keep it strong no matter what, over and over again, building it, keeping it, loving it.

There are so many beautiful things to love and this love had to start with me first. I learnt that by looking in the mirror I could tell myself how much I love everything about myself and how much I forgive myself for everything I have ever done and how amazing I am, and when I feel good, everything around me looks good, too. Then I celebrate, always celebrate, it makes you feel good, really good. It's that simple and easy.

As my self-love grew, I experienced more love radiating from me. I started to do the 50 foot rule, taught to me by the genius Joseph McClendon III. Wherever you are, whatever you are doing, you can play the 50 foot game. Focus on everyone within 50 feet of you and silently send them love from your thoughts. This is such a magical game and I have been doing this with my husband and our children, whether they are with me in the room or not, and the effect it has on them is beautiful. They magically feel the love. I can tell by their way of being. It helps them to shine.

So let's say there is a family challenge. I now choose to sit in love and radiate love out to each member of my family. I do a lot more observing than I ever did and a lot less speaking! I remember, God gave me two ears and one mouth, so I choose to listen twice as much as I speak.

I also use this technique globally, mentally holding the world in my arms, I send 6.9 billion people and all living things my love and gratitude, spreading this love over the entire world. We are so blessed to know the world is round and what it looks like shrunk into a ball size. I might have found this a little harder years ago!!!

Being in love with life is such a beautiful way of being. Everything looks so much more amazing when I have my "in love with life" eyes on! Everything shines, everyone shines, and I attract more amazing people and situations into my life. When I have my "in love with life" eyes on, I can see all the magic and the miracles that are in my life every day, every moment. Life is that simple -- looking through eyes of love and seeing just how stunning the world really is right now.

I am a member of my friend Jennifer Hough's "Heaven on Earth Construction Crew!" Dancing with what presents -- really dancing with what presents, every moment of every day, finding a way to love it all, no matter what. Being able to manage the present moment is beautiful and so fulfilling. One of the brilliant things about being in love is there are far fewer challenges. When I am in love and in joy my mind is a magnet and it attracts to it more love and joy. This is so awesome. I attract to me great things just by thinking loving thoughts! HOW EASY is that! When challenges arise, and they will because I need to grow (challenges are sent for us to grow our muscles!), I ask myself what lesson is it that I need to learn and grow from and how is this challenge challenging me?

Today we have snow, everything has slowed down and I am loving it. It meant that a charity walk for Kairos, a wonderful local charity I am supporting, was cancelled. But hey, we can reschedule that anytime in

I Am In Love With My Life

the new year and it gives us all more family home time. How special is that? Being flexible and dancing with what presents is beautiful. It helps transform every day into a success no matter what.

You can get into the mindset that everything is great right now, choosing being flexible and open to change and that everything is filled with love wherever you look, you'll find that it's magical and you will take this way of being with you wherever you go. Magical things will happen and life will feel beautiful and a stunning blessing - its the best feeling in the world. It makes life so fabulous. We really are living in Heaven on Earth right here right now, we have to recognise it, open our eyes to it. The more we recognise it the more it will expand for us.

So what am I going to do with all this love I have? It is my intention to keep on growing, pushing myself so that I have more to give, to be a shining light for my family and friends and keep on raising my bar! There is a saying: If you don't keep growing, you are starting to wither. And I don't do wither! So growing and learning is a must. It makes me feel good, (it will make you feel good too) and I love to celebrate my achievements all the time. It's so important to celebrate every day so that you feel good about what you achieve. That's a key component of feeling good and wanting to do more. Also remember to celebrate others' achievements too, it makes them feel great and you feel great.

I like to ask big questions. Something taught to me by Tony Robbins, another genius. Ask big questions and do not to settle until you get the answer. Keep going. Keep finding a way to make what you dream about work out for you. Always find another way, and then another way, to achieve success in every area of your life.

You need to have a dream, a passion, something that really gets you up in the morning. I have a big passion, I bet you do too. My number

Multiple Streams of Determination

one priority is looking after and growing me! I know that by treating myself well, looking after my wellness and vitality, my love and connection and my growth, I overflow to my loved ones around me. It's a bit like the airplane safety instructions that say take your own oxygen mask first, then give the masks to your children, this is not always a natural way of thinking, and yet its so obvious.

I put my darling husband, Michael, as my Number 2. I do everything I can for him. I do it with as much love and nurturing as I can possibly bring to our relationship. Michael is my biggest challenger! And the growth I have had as a result of being married to Michael is awesome. He is just what I need. We work on balance all the time, checking in on the love and connection we have and when we are both feeling loved up and fulfilled, and supporting each other, we can grow and contribute to each other and those around us. This takes practise every day, checking in and clearing up any messes we have created between us!!! The more we do it, the easier it gets, again its growing the muscles of understanding, compassion, forgiveness and so on. Learning to say sorry easily is vital in this love game. The more we share and connect, the deeper our love and connection grows and we both end up feeling more together and more valued and nurtured.

I like to think every day is a blank canvas. We can start over again! As the day goes on, only put things on there that matter in that moment always remembering to forgive fast, and forgiveness starts with myself and of course, with everyone around me, trying not to sweat the small stuff! So any difficult situations can be re-looked at every moment coming from a blank canvas of no meaning, no stories, lots of love and lots of focused thinking from my heart. I like to ask, "How can I really make a difference here and allow this situation to move on, so that we are working as a joyful team? How may I be of service here?"

I Am In Love With My Life

I learnt a lovely compassion exercise that I think you will find really helpful. It moves me each time I read it.

Objective: Increase the amount of compassion in the world. Expected results: A personal sense of peace.

Instructions: the exercise can be done anywhere that people congregate. It should be done on strangers unobtrusively, from some distance. Try to do all five steps on the same person.

> Step 1: With attention on the person, repeat to yourself, "Just like me, this person is seeking some happiness for his or her life."
>
> Step 2: With attention on the person, repeat to yourself, "Just like me, this person is trying to avoid suffering in his or her life."
>
> Step 3: With attention on the person, repeat to yourself, "Just like me, this person has known sadness, loneliness and despair."
>
> Step 4: With attention on the person, repeat to yourself, "Just like me, this person is seeking to fulfil his or her needs."
>
> Step 5: With attention on the person, repeat to yourself, "Just like me, this person is learning about life."

I totally love this exercise. It's so very magical. Imagine how stunning it would be if we all had this as our inner talk. The compassion around the world would be awesome.

I dream of a globally coherent world, a really globally coherent world, a world where we are all in balance, with ample good water and good food for all. I dream of a world where love and respect are just how we all are being 24/7. I know we all want the same, when we get right into our souls. We all want the love -- a loving, peaceful and harmonious world for all.

Multiple Streams of Determination

In May 2009, I came across a booth at The Mind Body Spirit Show in Victoria, London, for the Buddha Maitreya Shambhala Vajradhara Maitreya Sangha Monastery. I had tears of joy when I entered the booth and I had a really good feeling about what I had entered into. I felt, "Wow, this is what I have been looking for."

As it turns out, Buddha Maitreya is the reincarnation of all the Buddhas and of Jesus Christ. I told you I ask big questions – and that's how I found him. I had no idea that there was a living Jesus Christ -- not someone you meet every day! I bought all sorts of tools from the booth and filled our house with his sacred geometry. Then, as time has gone on, I have got more and more attracted to different tools and so interested in how these tools of his can help us all. Each tool assists us to come more into our hearts and some of the tools are so powerful that they are world healing tools -- how awesome is that -- taking the love out right across the world assisting Buddha Maitreya, Jesus Christ, with his work. I reckon I have a stunning assisting job.

I am really keen to be able to support Buddha Maitreya. At the moment, he is building a Shambhala Monastery in California for his Sangha, his nuns and monks. Shambhala means Heaven on Earth. Buddha Maitreya is a very tall, big man. He looks like a cuddly bear with a very generous heart. He is so not what I had expected. He is very American and very funny, a great combination. He lives a very humble life and sends money to all sorts of charities around the world, doing all sorts of amazing work. He has just been given some land in Lumbini, Nepal, where he is going to build his second Shambhala. We are raising £300,000, to build this monastery. Buddha was given a Plaque of Appreciation by the Government of Nepal.

The Shambhala monasteries are built on sacred geometry and have a massive impact on the energy of the world, opening us all up to more love. This is very cool.

In order to assist my life and to be able to better assist others around me, I have learnt the Law-of-Attraction-on-Steroids, a process taught by Joseph McClendon III at his seminar "The Next Step." It's so incredible. The process we are working on is winning multiple jackpots in the Euro Millions and the National Lottery, we plan to win a total of £100 million pounds this year. My plan is every time I win a jackpot, to give Buddha 50% of the jackpot. The other 50% we will use to build healing and learning centres to assist communities around the world to learn to become abundant in every area of their lives. These centres will be in memory of my darling family, to whom I am totally grateful. My life his been enriched by all the challenges that we shared.

I run a company called Dreamwork Developments, assisting others to catch their dreams and live a life they love. I wish for you to be at "The Next Step" and learn this magic for yourself. If you really have the desire to learn, call me and come to visit, and I will show you how it's done! We should all know this process from the moment we are able to learn anything at all. What a different world it would be.

If you have the ability to imagine, and we all have this ability, then the Universe has the ability and the resources to deliver it fully to you. The Universe is a well stocked kitchen with every ingredient we can imagine and even more than that!!!

I am sure it is now evident why I love my life. I have a beautiful and very wonderful family, and I have amazing dreams of how I can contribute to others globally -- and that makes me feel really good. Life is really very simple when you can appreciate just how lucky you are right now and how much you have to contribute. Remember, life is much easier and way simpler than we have been led to believe. Really, it is.

Multiple Streams of Determination

Put on the "in love with life" eyes and give yourself a gift. Life is a present. Enjoy this present right now. What are you waiting for?

Huge love and enormous hugs to you, love Georgie xoxoxo

I want to say a special thank you to Michael and to Carol Anne Cooper for their beautiful support over the writing of my chapter. Thank you darlings.

About the Author

Georgie lives in London with her darling soul mate Michael, a brilliant planning lawyer, and their two genius sons, Ollie and Henry. Georgie was brought up on a farm in Gloucestershire and had an idyllic childhood playing with all the animals, stunning green fields all around, with the space to be free and the freedom to spend hours lying in the fields looking up at the sky.

PASSIONS:

Georgie is passionate about health and nutrition, and by May 2011 will be certified by Joseph McClendon III as a wellness and vitality coach. Georgie loves to exercise and move her body and is training to run the 2012 London Marathon with her friend Jane Bailey. The aim is to raise £100,000 for the British Red Cross in memory of Georgie's darling mother Anne Verney, who died in January 2010. Georgie is passionate about life: "I am in love with life -- life is such a magical blessing."

BUSINESS:

Georgie stopped her interior decorating business of 23 years, The Chase Company, to become her mother's caregiver for the last magical five months of her life – a decision Georgie is deeply grateful for. Georgie has recently set up a new company called Dreamwork Developments.

I Am In Love With My Life

Georgie says: "I am so excited about Dreamwork Developments. I feel my heart sing with passion for the vision I have with this company. It is the product of all my dreams coming together, to be of outstanding service in the transformation of humanity, moving us all towards a globally coherent world. One of the things we are doing is assisting Buddha Maitreya in building monasteries around the world. By building these monasteries based on the existing Sacred Geometric Church of Shambhala Vajradhara Maitreya Sangha Monastery, a magnificent energy shift occurs across the earth assisting each and every one of us to open up our hearts. Can you imagine how different the world will look when we are all operating from our hearts, living lives we love and co-creating in a globally coherant life for all? How totally awesome is that. The first monastery has been built in Northern California and is the prototype for future monasteries. The second is soon to be built in Nepal. We are raising £300,000 to build the second monastery, which seems an amazingly small amount of money for such an auspicious project."

PURPOSE:

My life's purpose is to inspire each and every one of us to catch our dreams and to life a life we all love. Its our birthright to live amazing abundant lives full of love. Life is very simple and magical, and with co-creation, everything moves further faster, global coherence for us all one day soon.

Chapter 15

Unlimited Power

SEAN CONNER

Before I expose the most personal part of me to the world, I would first like to give all the thanks to my great God and savior, Jesus Christ, my mom and dad, and all of my homies who have supported and loved me unconditionally through good and bad! I also want to give a huge thanks to Johnny Wimbrey for making this possible and being the best mentor God could ever give me.

I was born in raised in a small town Murrells Inlet, South Carolina. I was raised in a well-off Christian home, and on the surface I enjoyed a pretty normal childhood that featured everyday sports and my handful of friends. However, I was put through challenges that nearly destroyed me. Instead, those challenges turned me into a rock-solid and unstoppable go-getter.

My passion in writing this is not to impress you, but to impress upon you and show you that we have the power to turn our worst situations

Multiple Streams of Determination

into the greatest life-changing experience. No matter the obstacles, we can live a purpose-driven life the way God wants us to live.

As I turned 21, I made a decision that I was no longer going to live limited by the opinions of others and the situation I had been given. Instead, I decided to start living with passion and fulfillment the way everyone deserves to live.

This is my story.

As I write this chapter, I realize I am exposing my deepest and most personal secret, one that could make me or destroy me. I hope you will be able to take this message and the lessons I've learned and apply them to your daily life.

As we start to replay my movie, I have the clear memory of being in the pediatrician's office 10 years ago. The doctor was saying that, although my condition was not life-threatening or health-threatening, it could create problems for me educationally and physically. I was also told that there is no cure and that I would have to live and deal with this condition for the rest of my life.

That was the day that, after much testing, I was diagnosed with Tourette syndrome, which is an inherited neuropsychiatric disorder. TS usually is detected in childhood, and is characterized by multiple physical or motor tics and at least one vocal tic.

I'd already been diagnosed with attention deficit disorder. My mom and dad were destroyed, and they hurt for my situation.

How does one get diagnosed with TS? For me it all started when I began mocking people with something that I would see on TV or that someone had done, usually because I thought it was funny. What I had done was unconsciously created a series of physical habits. Those habits soon led to a diagnosis that would lock in my mind an incurable neurological disease.

There was no blood testing. The diagnosis was based solely on my physical motions. Once diagnosed, I was then prescribed a medicine that was supposed to calm these habits, or tics, so I could focus on my school work and sports.

The complete opposite happened. This medicine put me on a downhill rollercoaster ride that took my case from moderate to severe. I had started out with very moderate noises or movement that no one would ever notice. The medicine took me to a state where I could not control myself. My arms and legs would jerk or flex constantly and I would make noises. If people saw or heard me, they thought I'd lost my mind.

As this became a constant day-to-day struggle, my mind was being programmed to continue these tics. When one would subside, another one would come. It was a roller coaster that never allowed me to get off. The only thing I thought about was how hard to hold on for the next drop or turn.

I remember lying in my bed one night after a horrible day. My soul was shattered. I was no longer the life-loving kid I used to be. As I lay there trying to fall asleep, my arm continued to jerk. If I focused hard enough, I could control it. But at that time I was too broken and tired to fight. As the sleepless night went on, I started to cry uncontrollably.

A series of questions streamed through my head. Why would God put me through this? How is this going to alter my life and my dreams? How am I going to hold my wife without the constant pressure of trying to be still?

As I finally fell asleep, I was angry at God and myself. I was giving up. Every day and night was like this. My mind was programmed to

Multiple Streams of Determination

give up. I was stuck with something I thought I would never be able to escape.

> *His disciples asked him, "Rabbi, who sinned, this man or his parents, that he was born blind?" "Neither this man nor his parents sinned," said Jesus, "but this happened so that the works of God might be displayed in him.*
> – John 9:2-3

This constant battle went on for years. After awhile I decided to get off all my prescription drugs. Getting off the drugs brought my tics and movements from severe back down to moderate. Although I was able to focus more on my school and socialize more, my soul was still left in pieces. I was lost, shattered, and confused, and the day-to-day tics still remained.

At the time, a guy by the name of Nick Vujicic was appearing all over the media. How inspiring he was. I sat and watched in pure amazement because Vujicic had no arms or legs! He was speaking to a crowd of about 400 people and bringing all of them to tears. This was a breakthrough for me. This guy who had no arms and no legs had joy pouring out of him, and he was in complete harmony with God. As I continued to watch, I saw him driving boats, swimming, playing soccer, and letting nothing stand in his way.

I experienced a personal breakthrough. Seeing Vujicic made me take a second look at myself. I was disgusted with myself for being so selfish and angry at God.

After this I found myself in the gym training intensely. Only this time, I paid attention to what my body was capable of doing. I have two working and very strong arms. I have hands that enable me to feel every surface that I touch. I have two powerful legs that move me wherever I want and let me experience speed.

Unlimited Power

I mentally went through the rest of my physical blessings. I went on to my eyesight, my hearing, and my voice. When we use these powerful gifts that God created for us, we often fail to realize that there are thousands of people who lack these gifts. Yet some of them are doing ten times what the average person is capable of doing. From then on I realized that I had been blessed with way more than I deserved.

My passion for God exploded, which sparked my enthusiasm for mission trips and spreading the Gospel of Christ to the lost. My personality and happiness came back tenfold. My whole outlook on life completely changed. All of my negative thoughts turned to positive, and before I could even realize it, my spirit had been renewed and I regained my confidence.

I made a decision that I was going to live life with a passion, and not to do anything unless it brought fulfillment. Many may ask, "Well, what about your Tourette syndrome? How are you still coping with that?" The fact is that having TS has been absolutely empowering.

Ten years ago a doctor diagnosed me with an incurable condition. The problem is that doctors around the country are diagnosing many people with this disease or that disease and leaving patients with no hope for a cure. They tell us that this is something we will have to live with the rest of our lives.

I refute that idea and throw my diagnosis out the window. I am disease-free and diagnosis-free. I am the way God intended me to be. There is no doctor or employer or anyone else who can convince me I don't deserve my life blueprint.

My TS case has been minimal for the past three years.

> *It's not what happens that determines your life future.*
> *It's what you do about what happens.*
>
> ~ Jim Rohn

Multiple Streams of Determination

Over the past year I have been coaching some of my closest friends when they come to me with troubles that are beating them down. I use with them an effective technique I've developed during the past few years in my evangelism. I've learned that it is ten times more powerful to ask questions that lead people to answers than just telling them the answers.

Perhaps you find yourself in a downward spiral. You see yourself as a failure, and you start to convince yourself that your dreams are not meant to be. You may question whether you're good enough, and doubt that you'll be the best at anything.

Fortunately, you don't have to stay on that spiral. Instead, start asking yourself what I call my Six Questions to Success.

1. What great lessons have I learned from failing?
2. How can I use these lessons to better myself at this task?
3. Though my goal is not yet accomplished, who or what makes me happy today?
4. Why does this person/thing/activity make me happy?
5. How does this happiness make me a better person?
6. How can this happiness help me accomplish this goal I am trying to obtain?

My point is here is that, instead of focusing on a negative, we need to change our mindset. We can use these questions in any situation. A failure is a failure today, not tomorrow. With each failure we can either mope and roll over or we can use it as a lesson to make ourselves better.

We also need to recognize who or what we have in our lives that make us happy. If we can be happy and thankful for what we have now, then we can use ourselves to our full ability to accomplish goals we have not yet accomplished. In my business I fail every day, and if I'm not getting the results I want or need at that particular moment, my happiness does not subside. Why? Because without my daily or yearly accomplishment, I still have my handful of people and things that make me happy. If I fail at my business does that mean I fail with God? Does that mean my family and friends will think less of me? What is it that we fear?

An example I like to use is the case of a friend whose financial life went down the drain in the matter of twelve months. One day as we talked, he told me how he was stressed to the max. I asked him my Six Questions to Success. Then I asked him if he was missing his arms or legs or if he was about to die. By the time he answered these questions, he realized that he still has a great life ahead of him, with or without the money he lost.

The lesson here is that so many of us live in fear and self-doubt. We don't recognize that a situation that appears full of doom might actually be an opportunity for unlimited success. For so long I looked at my diagnosis as a dead-end road that would shape and limit my life. I constantly lived in fear of my situation. It was not until I decided to face it head-on that I could become the strong person I am today. If I did not make the decision to change, I guarantee I would have not had the opportunity to relay this message to you and to others across the world.

So if you're reading this book, you're either one of those people who are living with passion or one of those people who are desperately looking for passion in their personal and spiritual life. My friends, I urge you to reach deep down inside yourselves to unleash the power within. Whether you're in a financial crisis and can't see a way out or you have an illness and feel there is no hope, you have the chance to make a life-changing decision and live life to its absolute fullest.

Multiple Streams of Determination

When we believe in ourselves we can achieve some incredible things. We can decide to stop living in the story we are in and create our own destiny. If you decided to make the decision to change, then put a smile on your face and get excited. Be thankful for your legs and run as fast as you can. Be thankful for your arms to hug your loved ones. And be thankful for your voice and use your words to tell the world you are a new person, and that you are no longer going to settle for less!

> *Good things come to those who wait, but great things come to those who take action!*
> ~ Sean Conner

About the Author

Sean is quickly becoming an influential force in his community and soon to be around the world. With his outgoing personality and passion for God he has gained a strong following who have always look forward to his future projects. While his former passion was in modeling and acting he has decided to take his passions to a much larger scale becoming an international speaker and author. Sean also plans to continue his Christian apologetic studies and continue bringing the gospel to the lost. Some of Sean's biggest influences include Anthony Robbins, Jim Rohn, and Jeff Durbin which he says is the perfect combination to learn how to live a passion fulfilled life. Brick by brick Sean is developing himself as a leader and plans to leave no searching soul behind.

For information about Sean please visit www.successwithsean.com

Chapter 16

From Corporation to Liberation

GEORGE ADAMIDES

I want to make a confession: I am just an ordinary guy.

I was brought up in a kind and supportive family, with all the ideas about how life, career and marriage should be. But among all the "you must do's" was a voice deep within me that was singing a different song, a song that gradually increased in volume until it covered all other music my family, my bosses, my friends and society were playing.

Before I proceed, I would like to express that I feel both honoured and humbled to have the opportunity to share my journey with you, and to be amongst some of the great teachers and mentors who have been my personal role models for years. Isaac Newton said, "If I have seen a little farther it is by standing on the shoulders of giants," and this also applies to me.

The Early Days

In my first years of life, doctors diagnosed me with rheumatic fever and I lost the use of one of my legs. I was told this illness would stay with me all my life. Through the power of prayer of my loved ones and with God's grace, I was miraculously healed.

My family and I moved to Australia when I was seven years old, as my father, who is a geologist, sought a better career opportunity.

The struggle we endured during those years will always remain vivid in my mind. My father worked for months on end in the middle of the West Australian desert in temperatures of more than 40 degrees Celsius (104 degrees Fahrenheit); my mother raised three children on her own whilst working in three jobs. They made these sacrifices in order to provide their children with the best opportunities in life. However, the hardships they endured never made sense to me: Why did it have to be so hard? These experiences strengthened my character and made me realize that God had a plan for me, a purpose to fulfil in this world.

Upon completion of school, like most young people, I didn't have a clue what I wanted to do with my life. I did what the masses did and enrolled at university. I quit after just a few months and worked in restaurants whilst I pondered my future path. I asked myself a simple question: "What do I love to do most?" When you ask quality questions you get quality answers, and the answer steered me in the direction of hotels and travel.

Make a decision of commitment

When I made a decision to study hotel management, I was committed to that. The word *decision* comes from the Latin word *decisio*, which means to cut off. This is exactly what I did; I cut off all alternatives.

Usually upon making major decisions, obstacles come along to test us.

One of the first obstacles was my parents disagreeing with me about moving to England in order to finish my degree. Most people just make plans - and I learned, sometimes the hard way, that plans change. But decisions don't. I asked another question: "How can I make it to the UK without the aid of my parents?"

Upon completion of my diploma in Cyprus, I applied to universities in England and for a personal loan, and I was both accepted and approved. Once my parents saw how determined I was, they supported me 100 percent. Life will always test us in how much we want something, and it is the individuals who persevere who will ultimately win, for the sheer reason that losing is not an option.

The Corporate World

I completed my degree in England and joined one of the top worldwide hotel chains as a graduate. Even though I had worked in four different luxury hotels whilst studying, I started from scratch in the UK hotel industry.

I urge anyone who is in, or looking to enter, the corporate world to find an employer that believes in him or her. You are the biggest asset they have, and if they are willing to invest in you through training, that's a huge part of winning the game. I had found a company whose core culture was to keep its employees happy, because happy employees will, in turn, keep customers happy and coming back which, in turn, keeps the shareholders happy. What an amazing philosophy!

Find a coach or mentor who is where you want to be

The first move this company made for me was to assign me a mentor. I would meet with my mentor monthly and receive ongoing sup-

Multiple Streams of Determination

port. I learned to see my weaknesses as development areas, to view problems as opportunities for growth, and to ask the right questions. I also learned the power of having a written plan. Finally, I understood that a mentor can collapse timeframes and accelerate the learning process.

In late 2003, my company sent me to a three-day seminar with the core idea being the power of positive thinking and the use of language. The quality of our relationships is directly related to the quality of our communication skills, and this individual was taking communication to a whole new level. Those three days shifted my mindset and changed my life forever. I began to invest in myself, and to read books to further understand how the mind works. I came to the conclusion that conventional education is enough to merely survive; I needed self-education if I were to thrive.

If there is no fear, there is no challenge

When I had the opportunity to move into the sales department I jumped at it. At the interview I was honest and confided to the general manager, "I'm definitely up for the challenge; however, I do have a sense of fear there. It's something completely new since my background is food and beverage."

He replied, "George, if there is no fear, there is no challenge, and if there is no challenge, what is the point?" He was right! I went for it and literally thrived in the following couple of years achieving some of the best sales results of all the London hotels in our chain.

I faced dramatic changes in my career when, due to financial reasons, I was left with no choice but to move companies. I got a wake-up call two months after moving, as I found myself in the limelight of corporate carnage; costs had to be cut and out of fourteen colleagues, two had to go. I was told I was safe; however two colleagues faced the dawn of a New Year, just as the recession sank in, with unemployment. My faith in the corporate system began to crack.

Due to my experience and ambition, I was appointed to a very good position in one of the top five-star resorts in the Mediterranean. For an ordinary guy like me this was considered a "dream job," especially as it entailed continuous travel to Europe and the Middle East. Even though in my mind I had a great sense of satisfaction, deep in my heart I felt unfulfilled. There was something missing.

It wasn't until I had been introduced to a totally different model of working, a concept of being rewarded according to the effort and results you produced, that I got it. I couldn't deny myself a part-time business, and getting involved for the first time in the entrepreneurial world was like love at first sight. I was captured! The flame for my career was fading, but a new, more intense fire began to burn. My father noticed that my focus was split into two, and one day, in a serious tone, explained, "George, a servant cannot have two masters." This is when I realised I had to make another decision.

It is hard to believe how a single defining moment can shape your entire future. Without hesitation I left behind a career I'd spent 10 years building, like an old suit I didn't want to wear any more. I sat and calculated how many months of funds I had to survive; it totalled around four. I then gave my resignation. This was completely out of character. I was asked, "What more was I looking for?" My manager thought that I was having a breakdown and asked me to sleep on it; my family believed that I had lost my mind. The truth was, I had a burning desire to follow my dreams and this was not allowing me to take any other route. I jumped and grew my wings on the way down.

Multiple Streams of Determination

The Entrepreneurial World

In the first few weeks of my self-employment I had to confront my fear and hesitations. My mind panicked as all the worst case scenarios were visualised in my mind. I had moved way out of my comfort zone. Having a job gives you a sense of security, even though a lot of the time it is an illusion. Suddenly, I felt naked. I had only one person ever to report to again - myself! As scary as this was, it also brought with it a greater sense of freedom and liberation than I had felt for a very long time. I was the master of my fate, I was the captain of my ship; it all started and ended with me! I felt in the core of my being that this was the right thing and knew I was going to make it happen. I left myself no other option. I burned the bridge behind me.

One of the saddest things we find in today's world is that so many people neither have the strength nor the willpower to sail away and lose sight of the shore. Yet, isn't this the only way to discover new land?

There is a lie that has been passed down for generations that exceptional things can only be achieved by super heroes. In a depressed economy, are there people who are increasing their lifestyle and achieving great things? Absolutely! What are they doing differently? I believe a part of the answer is that they choose not to move with the masses, and through sheer willpower and determination decide to do as salmon do, to swim against the current, to move upstream.

Our darkest moments possess the seeds for our greatest victories

My fears were manifested as I faced my darkest moment in December 2009. Money was not coming in and I was struggling. As the unpaid bills and unopened red letters were piling up, I began questioning myself. I realise now this is common when you start your own business.

Defining Moments

I will never forget the stormy evening I was driving one of my closest friends to the airport. The rain was pouring down and I had to drive carefully as my tyres were so bald that if I braked too hard, my car would simply slide. She was the only one, besides my sister, who knew the depth and seriousness of the situation I was facing. Upon saying goodbye to her at the airport café and sharing an extended final hug, she told me she'd left some money in my bag in the car in order to support me through the next few weeks. I stared into her eyes speechless whilst my eyes welled up. Deep inside me I felt crushed and began crying uncontrollably on her shoulder. I felt a deep sense of embarrassment and shame at how desperate my situation had become. I was so successful in my career, but look at me now.

As I stood there waving goodbye, alone and petrified, at the same time I was filled with deep gratitude at my friend's kindness as her generosity would help me to survive for a few more weeks. My prayers had been answered and once again I experienced how God works in miraculous ways to help us.

I always knew that after the storm a rainbow follows. My father lent me the money to replace all my tyres and things slowly began to change for the better. I was back on the road and successfully passed yet another test. One year later, I have various streams of income, customers and business partners in fifteen different countries and an expanding business. I've travelled on nine holidays, attended seminars for my own personal growth in Cyprus, Italy, UK, and the US, and I've trained as a professional speaker.

I now own my life.

Never listen to dream stealers

One of the keys to my success was my resilience and my ability to con-

Multiple Streams of Determination

front my feelings whilst disciplining my emotions and fears. Yet one of my greatest allies was the ability to ignore the people on the sidelines, or "dream stealers," as one of my mentors likes to call them. People who are not on the field playing the game do not deserve to be heard. As Martin Luther King said, "Faith is taking the first step, even when you don't see the whole staircase."

I took that first step and found the individuals along the way who shared the same vision as I did. If you can't find a winning team, then create one. There is nothing more powerful than a handful of people who share the same vision. My brother Andreas inspired me from a young age with his entrepreneurial spirit. However, it was my sister Efrosyni who shared this vision with me. Her support and guidance made the transition from the corporate world to the Promised Land so much easier.

It was not easy, of course. Actually, it is the most challenging thing I have ever done. For the first time in my life, I had to fight against the worst opponent a man can confront - myself, my own fears, my limiting beliefs, my insecurities. I lost the battle so many times, I can't describe to you or give you the full story in a few lines. But in the end, I won the war.

The rewards are beyond my wildest expectations, and for those who also hear that voice deep inside them, I wish for you one day to experience the same. It's not about the money. It is about the person I had to become to deserve a quality lifestyle of wealth and freedom.

Never never never quit!

As children we have been taught that every story "must have" a happy ending. Well, this ending was purposely designed via my decisions. Truthfully, I feel that this is actually my beginning. I cannot dare to imagine how my life would be if at any moment I simply said, "I give up!"

I couldn't give up. I had put all my chips on the table, all my dreams were wrapped around one decision, one defining moment. What could I give up? It's my life we are talking about! I was so determined that even during those dark days, I couldn't betray my own self. You see, in life there is always a price you have to pay. Either you pay the price of perseverance or the price of regret. The difference is that perseverance weighs ounces whereas regret weighs tons. I chose, and I choose, to persevere.

As I told you, I'm just an ordinary guy. As William Halsey rightly said, "There are no extraordinary men, just extraordinary circumstances that ordinary men are forced to deal with."

About the Author

George Adamides is an unstoppable individual with a unique gift in marrying his ten years corporate experience with an entrepreneurial spirit.

Upon earning a diploma with merit in Cyprus and a Bachelor of Science degree with commendation in England, George was accepted, from almost three thousand applicants, for one of fifty positions with a top international hotel chain. He achieved accelerated success earning six promotions within five years and fast-tracking to management. Positions held include team leader of a food and beverage department with more than thirty employees in the biggest UK hotel of his chain outside of London. He also was the youngest regional business development manager for a large hotel and venue chain in the UK, and international sales manager for one of the finest five star resorts in the Mediterranean.

George decided at the end of 2009 to diversify and took the entrepreneurial route and has now successfully generated multiple streams of

Multiple Streams of Determination

income. He has provided training and spoken in universities, to corporations, and consulted for various firms in areas ranging from increasing customer satisfaction, sales and marketing, international expansion, developing peak performance and shifting the team mindset to achieve success.

George now travels the world speaking, training and motivating individuals to make decisions of commitment focused at improving their business and personal lives. His passion, warmth and openness inspires and moves audiences, creating the belief and desire in themselves that, they too, can and deserve to achieve greatness.

Feel free to contact George Adamides on +357 99 533486 or at george@adamides.net for more information, or visit www.GeorgeAdamides.com.

Chapter 17

Defining Moments

JIM ROHN

(Introduction)

Over the last 38 years, spanning almost four decades, this individual has influenced people that have trained a whole class of personal development students. People like Mark Victor Hansen, Anthony Robbins, and more.

He's the author of dozens of books and cassettes, courses on success, on living a life that is your potential, and realizing your dreams.

Tonight, I will bring to you, the one, the only, Jim Rohn. Author of many books I've talked about. Tonight we're going to go A to Z on how you can live a life of success in business and in family.

Multiple Streams of Determination

How do you do that?

Why is he the mentor for millions of people worldwide?

(To Jim)

Jim Rohn, my dime, your dance floor. Welcome to The Mike Litman Show.

Hey, thanks Mike. I'm happy to be here.

Great. I know myself and everyone is very excited for you to share some wisdom tonight and talk about the concept of success and about the principles for achieving it in our next 57 minutes together.

I'd like to start out by defining the word. What does 'success' mean to Jim Rohn?

Well, I think the ultimate success, which I teach in my seminar, is living a good life.

Part of it is income. Part of it's financial independence Part of it is objectives that you achieve, dreams coming true, family, children, grandchildren, good friends, productivity. It's a wide range.

It's all encompassing, the word "success".

It's not just your job, your income, your fortune. Not just your paycheck or your bank account. But everything. From all of your achievements during your life to trying your best to design a way to make it all give you a good life.

So, we're talking about design. We'll get to ambition.

We're talking about goals. We're talking about planning. You talk about something in your literature.

You mention that success doesn't need to be pursued. It needs to be attracted.

Defining Moments

What do you mean by that?

That's true.

I was taught, starting at age 25 when I met a mentor of mine by the name of Mr. Shoaff. He taught me that success is something you attract by the person you become. You've got to develop the skills.

He talked about personal development: become a good communicator, learn to use your own language.

He talked about the management of time.

But primarily developing yourself, your attitude, your personality, developing your own character, your reputation. Then developing the skills. From sales skills to recruiting skills, to management skills, leadership skills, how to work with a variety of people. You know, the full list.

He taught me to work on myself, because I used to work on my job.

He said, "If you work on yourself, you can make a fortune." That turned out to be true for me.

He turned it all around and said, "success is not something you run after, like a better job."

Although that is to be desired.

You've just got to ask yourself, "am I qualified for doubling, tripling, multiplying my income by three, four, five?"

If I look at myself and say, "No, not really." Then I need to ask myself, "Who could I find?

Where can I go that could pay me three, four, five times as much money?"

Multiple Streams of Determination

Then, you have to say, "at the present there probably isn't anyone. I can't just fall into a lucky deal."

But, if I went to work on myself immediately. Work on my attitude, personality, language, and skills. Then that begins the process of attracting the good job, the good people, and building a business or creating a career that could turn out to make you financially independent, perhaps wealthy.

Jim, so really what we are talking about is a change of mindset. Of changing our thinking and getting in tune with the universe.

Talk about something that you mentioned. Changing your language. Describe what that means.

There is the language that can fit.

You can use careless language around home and around the community.

But, if you want to start stepping up, then you've got to learn the language. The corporate language. You've got to learn the sales language.

Then you've got to be careful not to be careless with your language in the marketplace. It can cost you too much.

You know, a guy that is inclined to tell dirty stories, inclined to use a bit too much profanity. It might be okay in the inner circle and at the bar or whatever. But when you start to move into the world of business and finance where you want to be successful, earn a better paycheck, move up the scale, you just have to be careful. So, one of the major things is your language.

Not just that, but learning the language of success. Learning how to treat people with respect. Giving people inspiration when they need it, correction when they need it.

Defining Moments

The same thing as learning to work with your children.

Language opens the door for fortune. It opens the door for help. It opens the door for better living. It opens the door for a good marriage. It opens the door for a stable friendship.

A big part of it starts with our thinking, our attitude, and then a major part of it is the language we use.

Okay, something that we are sharing tonight with people worldwide now, is we are talking about an inner change, then the outer result.

So many times people are trying to change the outer, without changing the inner. Is that what we are talking about?

Yeah, that's true.

The big part of it, of course, is to start with philosophy.

Making mistakes and judgments can just cost you so much in the marketplace, at home, with your family, whatever it is. Errors in judgment can really do us in. It can leave us with less of a life than we could've had.

We've got to learn to correct those errors whether they are errors in philosophy or something else.

My mentor asked once why I wasn't doing well.

I showed him my paycheck and I said, "This is all the company pays." He said, "well, that's really not true. With that philosophy, you'll never grow."

I said, "No, no, this is my paycheck. This is all the company pays." So, he said, "No, no,

Multiple Streams of Determination

Mr. Rohn. This is all that the company pays you."

I thought, 'wow, I'd never thought about that.'

He said, "doesn't the company pay some people two, three, four five times this amount?" I said, "well yes." He said, "then this is not all that the company pays. This is all that the company pays you."

For your income to multiple by three, four, five, you can't say to the company, "I need more money." You've just got to say to yourself, 'I need a correction in my philosophy. I can't blame circumstance. I can't blame taxes. I can't say it's too far, too hot, too cold. I've got to come to grips with myself.'

That is really where it all begins.

It's corrections of errors in judgment and in your own philosophy.

We're talking about philosophy. Is it really like ironing down a purpose?

You're talking about the word "philosophy" to someone listening right now and they're trying to put it into actual practice.

Someone right now that's in a rut, lost, how do you go about the process of putting together a philosophy that excites you and that benefits others?

You start with the easy stuff.

Ask most people, "What is your current philosophy for financial independence that you're now working on?", and usually the person says, "Gosh, I never thought about that."

Unless you have an excellent financial philosophy that gives you guidance to correct errors, accept some new disciplines, and make some changes, you can forget being financially independent.

Defining Moments

Ask yourself, "What is your philosophy on good health?" Is it to cross your fingers and sort of let it go and if something goes wrong then you fix it?

The answer is, no. You should try to learn up front.

Ask yourself, "What is your cholesterol count?" The average guy's philosophy is, 'I don't know and I don't care. If something goes wrong, I will try to fix it.'

But, by then usually it's too late. Now it'll cost you a fortune. It costs you time. Maybe even it costs you your life.

If someone can help you with errors in judgment, or help you correct your financial philosophy, your spiritual philosophy, your philosophy on a good relationship, that's where it all begins.

We go the direction we face, and we face the direction we think.

It's the things we think about and ponder. What are your values? What's good? What's not so good? What's the better way? What's the best way?

Unless we do some constructive thinking on that, we usually take the easier way.

Easy causes drift, and drift causes us to arrive at a poor destination a year or five years from now.

So, we're talking about increasing our self-awareness. We're talking about philosophy.

I want to transition to a concept of planning, but before I do, Jim, let's talk about something you have been talking about for decades.

You give people options and you give people a choice.

Multiple Streams of Determination

You say, "You can either be in somebody else's plan or playing in your own life." Can you talk about that?

That's true. Some people sort of resign to letting somebody else create the productivity, create the business, create the job, and it seems to be easier for them to punch the clock and let everyone else have the responsibility. Then they go home and try to make the best of it.

But, I think it is also good to start pondering and thinking, 'how could I take charge of my own life? Or whether I qualify for a better position where I am. Or whether I might create my own business, start something, developing from my personal productivity.'

If we just sit back and not take responsibility, that is what happens. Then we fit into someone else's plans, rather than designing plans of our own.

If you don't have plans of your own to fill that vacuum, you're probably going to fit into someone else's plan.

Jim, what if you don't know what the plan is?

What happens to someone when they're at a job right now, 9 to 5, working the clock, they don't know what they're passionate about, they don't know where to go, where do they start?

You don't have to operate from passion to begin with. You operate from necessity. My friend, Bill Bailey, said when he got out of high school he went to Chicago from

Kentucky and the first job he could find was night janitor.

Someone asked him, "how come you settled for a job as night janitor?" He said, "malnutrition."

So, the first passion is to survive. To somehow make it.

Defining Moments

Then start to build from there with something that you could find to do even if it is distasteful.

You don't have to love what you do. Just love the chance or the opportunity to begin the process. Because where you begin is not where you have to end a year from now, five years from now, ten years from now.

You just begin, first of all, to correct errors.

Find something, anything, it doesn't matter what.

America is such an incredible country especially. The ladder of success is available for everybody.

If you have to start at the bottom and make your way to the top, who cares? As long as they let you on the ladder.

Then, if you study, and grow, and learn, and take classes, and read books, burn a little midnight oil, start investing some of your own ambition, I'm telling you, the changes can be absolutely dramatic.

That is what happened for me starting age 25.

At age 25, in a six-year period, you went from being broke to becoming a millionaire.

Obviously, you put this stuff into practice. You started your own, I'll use the words, "mental make over", changing your thoughts, changing your attitude.

It seems to me, and this is personal for me, Jim, this quote of yours influences me tremendously even today, "discipline versus regret."

Talk about the importance of that. Talk about how to live a disciplined life and stay disciplined so you can get what you want.

It is true. We suffer one of two things. Either the pain of discipline or

Multiple Streams of Determination

the pain of regret. You've got to choose discipline, versus regret, because discipline weighs ounces and regret weighs tons.

Say that again.

Discipline weighs ounces and regret weighs tons.

The reason is because the regret is an accumulated affect a year from now, two years from now. When you didn't do the easy discipline.

It's like having a cavity in your tooth. The dentist says, "if we fix it now it's only $300, and if you let it go someday it's going to be $3,000."

So, the easier pain of the $300 and sitting in the chair for just a little while takes care of it.

But, if you let it go that's no good.

You know, the dentist says, "this cavity is not going to get better by itself. This is something you have got to take care of. You can't cross your fingers and hope it's going to go away.

That's not going to help."

Whatever you see that needs to be corrected, you start taking care of it.

If you don't have a splendid diet, you've got to be incredibly thoughtful about how to change that.

If your kids don't have a splendid diet, you've got to say, "Hey, maybe I should give some attention to my kids and their diet."

Nutrition affects behavior I was taught at age 25. Nutrition affects learning. Nutrition affects performance. Nutrition affects vitality. Nutrition affects decision-making. Nutrition affects longevity.

My mother studied and practiced good nutrition and talked to me about it, an only child, and my father too, who lived to be 93.

Defining Moments

The doctor told me that my mother extended her life at least 20 years by paying attention to nutrition and practicing the art.

The benefits are so incredible by taking a look at a few simple disciplines.

You know, if mom said, 'an apple a day', and the guy says, 'well, no. I'm not into the apple a day, I've got my fingers crossed and I think everything is going to be okay.', you've just got to say, 'this is a foolish person.'

It doesn't matter what it is. You don't have to take giant steps at first.

To have an incredible increase in self-esteem, all you have to do is start doing some little something. Whether it is to benefit your health, benefit your marriage, or to benefit your business, or your career.

You can eat the first apple of the new apple a day philosophy along with some other things you have decided to do. You could say one of these days I will never be healed again. I'm going to have all the breath I need. I'm going to have all the vitality I need. I'm munching on the first apple.

You don't have to revolutionize all at once. Just start.

But, the first apple you eat, if it's a plan to better health, I'm telling you, by the end of that first day your self-esteem starts to grow.

Say to yourself, 'I promise myself I'll never be the same again.'

It doesn't take a revolution. You don't have to do spectacularly dramatic things for self-esteem to start going off the scale. Just make a commitment to any easy discipline. Then another one and another one.

It doesn't take but just a collection of those new easy disciplines to start giving you the idea that you're going to change every part of your life: financial, spiritual, social.

Multiple Streams of Determination

A year from now, you'll be almost unrecognizable as the mediocre person you may have been up until now. All of that can change.

It doesn't change over night. But, it does change with a change in thought and philosophy. Pick up a new discipline and start it immediately.

When you bring up action, like Jack Canfield on the show a while ago talking about the universe rewards action, we talked about the concept of doing it personally. We can both concur on this, amazing things happen.

Those little baby steps create momentum. They create energy, force, and they create something that I want to steer back to.

You talk a lot about ambition, the fuel of achievement. You talk about being ambitious.

I personally saw my life revolutionized when I found something that I enjoyed and made it a necessity to be ambitious about it.

Talk about the power of ambition. How do we build a life where we become ambitious?

Sometimes ambition just lingers below the surface. All of the possibilities for ambition are there.

But, if you live an undisciplined life drifting on health, drifting on relationships, drifting on developing a better career, if you're drifting, it doesn't taste good at the end of the day. But, if you start something, I promise you, not only will you feel better about yourself in terms of self esteem, which develops self confidence, which is one of the greatest things in stepping towards success, it'll also start awakening a spark of ambition.

A person who has never sold anything in their life. Finally they get a product they can believe in. They make the first sale and all of a sudden they say, "gosh, if I did this once, I can do it again."

By the time they've made the 10th sale they say, "this could be the career for me. It could be the steps I need to become a leader. To become a giant in my field."

All of that stuff has the potential of awakening your ambition. To make the flames start to burn. It starts to grow.

But, it just doesn't grow unless you start the process.

You can't just say, "I'm praying and hoping that ambition will cease me tomorrow morning and everything will change."

Just start with some little something to prove to yourself that you're going to develop a whole list of disciplines.

Start with the easy ones first. It doesn't matter. Like making the necessary contacts in whatever business you're in.

If you make three phone calls a day, in a year that's a thousand.

Three does not sound like much. But, in a year it's a thousand.

If you make three positive calls a day, if you make a thousand positive calls, something phenomenal is going to happen to your life.

I also teach that the things that are easy to do are easy not to do.

If you want to learn a new language, three words a day, at the end of the year it gives you a vocabulary of a thousand words.

It's just easy to, but it's easy not to.

It's easier to hope it will get better than to start the process of making it better.

Multiple Streams of Determination

That is really the theme of my seminars.

(To the listeners)

On the topic of seminars, go to jimrohn.com to find out more about Jim's seminars. When you go to jimrohn.com subscribe to his newsletter.

There are tons of people that Jim has influenced and you'll hear the information tonight.

(Back to Jim)

Talk about the power, simplicity, and importance of having strong reasons.

That's major. If you have enough reasons, you can do anything.

If you have enough reasons, you'll read all the books you need to read.

If you have enough reasons, enough goals, enough objectives, enough things that you want to accomplish in your life, you'll attend whatever classes you need to attend. You'll get up however early you need to get up.

Sometimes we find it a little hard to get out of bed. We want to linger. Part of that is not just being tired, or weary, or a little bit of poor nutrition, some of it is just lack of the drive in terms of having a long enough list of reasons to do it.

Then you've just got to let the reasons grow. Things you thought were important this year, you go for them, then next year you look back and you say, "I was a little foolish about that. Here's what I really want. That isn't really important to me anymore." Then you just keep up this process of what's important to you.

Defining Moments

For your family, build a financial wall around your family nothing can get through. I made that statement, about six years ago, to a young couple that has twins. Fabulous. They now earn about five to six million dollars a year.

I remember the day they came to me and said, "You know that statement you made about building a financial wall around your family that nothing can get through? Well, we resolved to do that. Now we're happy to report to you that we have just crossed the line. We have now finished building the financial wall around our family nothing can get through."

I'm telling you, the power of something like that is amazing. That's just a small example of all the things that can inspire your life.

Where do you want to go? Who do you want to meet? How many skills do you want to learn this year? How many languages do you want to learn?

I go and lecture in the Scandinavian countries. They all speak four or five, six languages.

In the school system you are required to learn four languages. Three they assign, and one you can pick.

I mean, there isn't anything you can't do in terms of language, skills, business, financial independence, or being a person of benevolence.

The famous story of Latorno, back when I was a kid, was an inspiring story. He finally got to the place where he could give away 90% of his income.

My mentor, Mr. Shoaff, knew the story and said to me, "wouldn't that be great for you, Mr. Rohn? To finally get to the place where you could give away 90%?" I thought, 'wow that would be incredible.'

159

Multiple Streams of Determination

Somebody says, "90%. Wow that's a lot to give away." Well, you should have seen the 10% that was left. It was not peanuts.

But anyway, those kinds of dreams, those kinds of goals are what really start the fire. At first you just need the goals that start triggering activity immediately.

Say, "I want to be able to pay my rent on time within 90 days. I'm putting in a little extra time. I'm doing this, I'm doing that. I'm taking the class. Whatever. After 90 days, I'm never going to be late on my rent again. I'm tired of the creditors calling. What are my goals?"

I heard a knock on my door back when I was about 24. I went to the door and there was a Girl Scout selling cookies. She gives me the big pitch. Girl Scouts, best organization in the world, we've got this variety of cookies, just $2.00. Then, with a big smile, she asked me to buy.

I wanted to buy. That wasn't a problem. Big problem, though, was I didn't have $2.00 in my pocket.

I was a grown man. I had a family. A couple of kids. I had been to college one year. I didn't have $2.00 in my pocket.

I didn't want to tell her I was that broke. So, I lied to her and said, "Hey, I've already bought lots of Girl Scout cookies. Still got plenty in the house."

So, she said, "Well, that's wonderful. Thank you very much," and she left.

When she left, I said to myself "I don't want to live like this anymore. How low can you get?

Lying to a Girl Scout. I mean, that's about as low as you can go."

SO, that became an obsession for me.

Defining Moments

From that day on I said, "I'm immediately going to acquire whatever it takes to have a pocket full of money so that no matter where I am for the rest of my life, no matter how many Girl Scouts are there, no matter how many cookies they've got to sell, I'll be able to buy them all."

It just triggered something.

Now, that's not a ranch in Montana. That's not becoming a billionaire. But, it was enough of an incentive to get me started.

Shoaff taught me that you have to carry money in your pocket. He said, "$500 in your pocket feels better than $500 in the bank."

I couldn't wait 'til the moment when I had $500 in my pocket.

It doesn't take much to get started. Then the list goes on from there.

Then if you have enough of those reasons, don't tell me you won't get up early, stay up late, read the book, listen to the cassette, do the deal, take notes, keep a journal, work on your language, or work on your skills.

I'm telling you, it's all wrapped up there: dreams, visions, setting goals, starting with something simple.

When you talk about reasons, Jim, don't many of those strong reasons come out of a pain in one's life?

Sure.

Okay. Because I know from my own life that it can come from necessity and it can come out of pain and trying to get away from that.

The pain of not having $2.00 was pain enough.

Nobody else witnessed it, but me and the Girl Scout. Of course, I'm sure she didn't notice it because she accepted my lie and moved on.

Multiple Streams of Determination

But, I said, "I don't want this to happen anymore."

It was such an incredible resolve and it was only over $2.00. But it doesn't matter what it is.

If it's something you want to correct, something you never want to happen again, that's the beginning.

You're well known internationally about the power of goals, the key formula for success.

Can you tell us about goals? The importance of goals, but more specifically, how do you set them?

Do you think them? Do you write them down? Can you walk us through the power and the process of

goal setting?

In my two-day leadership seminar, I go through a little workshop. It's called Designing The

Next Ten Years.

It's really a simple process.

Start making lists of what you want.

I teach the simple, simple ways. Others have got some complicated ways of setting goals

and deadlines and all that stuff. I don't do that.

I just say to make a list of the books you want to read. Make a list of the places you want to

go. Start making a list of the things you wish to acquire.

Defining Moments

What kind of education do you want for your family? Make a list. Where are the place you want to visit? Make a list.

What kind of experiences do you want to have? Make a list.

Decide what you want. Then write it all down. Put a lot of little things on there so you can start checking some things off. Because part of the fun of having the list is checking it off. No matter how small it is.

My first list had a little revenge. Some of the people who said I couldn't do well. They went on my list. I couldn't wait to get my new car and drive it up on their lawn. A few little things on revenge.

It doesn't matter what it is. It's your personal list. You can tear it up and throw it away if you want and then get started on it.

Later you can say as you look back, "I was all hot on this idea. Now, here's something I know that is much better. I'm going to forget about that other thing." So, it's an ongoing, continual process.

But, I have discovered that if you think about the things you want" for you, your family, some goals are individual, some are collective, some are family, some are business, just start with that. Rearrange it any way you want to. You don't have to have any deadlines. You can look at the list after you've made it and start putting a 1, 3, 5 or 10 number beside each item. You know, "I think I can accomplish that in about a year. I think I can accomplish that in about three years. I think I can accomplish that in about five years." Something like that. But, it's easy.

Success is easy. Especially in America it's easy. Bangladesh, it's hard. Cambodia, it's hard. America, it's easy.

If you don't believe that, if you think easy is hard, then you are in trouble all your life.

Multiple Streams of Determination

We've got to teach our kids. Some of them have the concept that America is hard. They don't understand the difference between Bangladesh and America.

The average income in Bangladesh is about $100 a year. That's what's hard.

If you understand what's hard and what's easy, you can say, "Wow, it ought to be easy here."

The only reason for not doing well here, is not applying yourself for some information to learn, and then start to practice right away.

You've got to practice. You have to do the deal. You read this book on good health, right?

It talks about nutrition and it talks about exercise then in the middle of the book the author says, "Now reader, set this book aside. Fall on the floor and see how many push ups you can do." Then, of course, you don't do that. So, you read on and the author says, "If you didn't set this book aside and if you didn't fall on the floor to see how many push ups you can do, why don't you just give this book away? Why bother yourself with reading if you're not going to pick an idea and try it?"

That's such great advice.

Ok, I want to bring something up and see if you agree with me on it.

We're talking about taking action. We're talking about planning, ambition, and taking those baby steps.

It seems to me, in my own personal life, when you start taking the steps, start changing your thinking, start moving forward toward a dream or vision, it almost seems like the universe conspires with you to help you. Do you see that as well?

Defining Moments

Absolutely!

A phrase in the Bible seems to indicate that whatever you move towards, moves towards you.

It mentions that God said, 'if you make a move toward me, I'll make a move toward you.'

If you move toward education, it seems like the possibilities of education start moving your way.

If you move toward good health, the ideas for better health, the information starts moving toward you.

That's good advice.

If you'll just start the process of moving toward what you want, it is true, mysteriously, by some unique process, life loves to reward its benefactors.

If you start taking care of something, it wants to reward you by producing and looking well.

If you take care of flowers, they seem to bloom especially for you and say, "Look how pretty we are. You have taken such good care of us. Now we want to give back to you by giving you our beauty."

I taught my two girls how to swim and dive. Of course, like all kids, they'd say, "Daddy, watch me. Watch me do this dive." It's almost like they're saying, 'You're the one that taught me. You're the one that had patience with me. You invested part of your life in this process.

Now watch me. Watch how good I am.'

All of life wishes to do that. All life wishes to reward its benefactor.

Multiple Streams of Determination

It could be something like a garden that grows because you took the time to cultivate it, to pull out the weeds, and take care of the bugs. Now, the garden does extremely well for you as a reflection back to you Because you are the one that invested time, energy, effort, and a piece of your life.

Let's stay here, Jim. Talk about the power of giving and the word "tithing". Can we talk about giving and what happens when someone gives?

I teach a little formula for kids called seventy, ten, ten, and ten.

This formula is about never spending more than 70 cents out of every dollar you earn.

The way it works is that ten cents is for active capital, ten cents is for passive capital, and then ten cents is to give away.

Whether it's to your church, a benevolent organization, or whether you let someone else manage it, or you manage it yourself.

We've got to teach generosity right from the beginning. I teach that ten percent is a good figure to start with.

You know when you become rich and wealthy, it can be 20, 30, 40, 50, 60, 70, 80, 90.

Whatever.

But, ten cents is the start.

If you teach generosity, I'm telling you, kids will give you a dime out of every dollar to help someone that can't help themselves.

It's about what it does for you spiritually. Do it for what it brings back to you in terms of self- esteem.

Defining Moments

Help to enrich the world by giving, and not only 10 percent of your money, but maybe some percentage of your time as well.

That investment is a smart investment.

It may bring returns to you immediately in ways you don't even know. It can do amazing things for your character, your reputation, and your inner spirit. It's all worth it!

Someone might say, "Well, I gave to this organization and they misused it."

It doesn't matter to you whether they misused it or not. The key for you is that you gave. They've got to be responsible on there own side.

No matter what though, giving is a major piece. Then, the next step is giving somebody your ideas.

This mentor, I met when I was 25, Earl Shoaff is someone I have to thank for the rest of my life for taking the time to share with me a bit of his philosophy that revolutionized my life.

I was never the same again after the first year. No one has ever had to say to me after the first year I was with him, 'when are you going to get going? When are you going to get off the dime?'

I've never heard that since that first year that I met this man who gave me his ideas and he did it freely.

He did it with great excitement. Because he knew that if he invested in me, I would probably invest in someone else.

Sure enough, that turned out to be true.

Ok. It's been 38 years or so. You're entering your second decade of doing this.

Multiple Streams of Determination

Where does the continuous passion and inspiration come from for you? Why are you still doing this?

It's very exciting because it's made me several fortunes and continues to do so.

But, part of the greatest excitement is when your name appears in somebody's testimonial.

You know, someone says something like, "I was at a certain place in my life and I listened to this person and it changed my life.

Mark Hughes, the founder of HerbaLife, used to say that because he attended my seminar when he was 19 it changed his life. He said, "I attended Jim Rohn's seminar and he was the first person that gave me the idea that in spite of my background I could make changes and become successful."

You can imagine how that made me feel. It's amazing for me to have my name appearing in his testimonial.

But, whether it's Mark Hughes or someone else, it doesn't matter.

Imagine this scenario: You've got someone who says, "Let me introduce you to the person that changed my life five years ago. We were sitting at Denny's five years ago and he recommended this book to me. He told me that it has really helped him. SO, he recommended it to me. Well, as I look back on it now, that was the beginning of some incredible life changes for me. Look where I am today. I'm telling you, it started five years ago at Denny's on a

Tuesday morning when this person introduced me to this book."

So, you don't have to give seminars. You don't have to give lectures. You don't even have to write books to affect someone's life and to do it

Defining Moments

so well that your name appears in their testimonial someday.

You know, someone says, "Here's the person who believed in me until I could believe in myself. Someone who saw more in me than I could see at the beginning."

Let's stay here, Jim. Because there's something I want to get across to people. It's such a powerful a statement that you talk about. I've heard you talk about the concept of sure, we want to reach our destination. We want to reach our goals. But, more importantly, Jim, can you talk about the power in the being and the becoming?

Well, true. What we acquire of course is valuable. But, the greatest value is not what we acquire. The greatest value is what we become.

My mentor had an interesting way of teaching it. When I was 25 years old he said, "I suggest, Mr. Rohn, that you set a goal to become a millionaire."

I was all intrigued by that. You know, it's got a nice ring to it - millionaire.

Then he said, "Here's why…" I thought to myself, 'gosh, he doesn't need to teach me why.

Wouldn't it be great to have a million dollars.' Then he said, "no then you'll never acquire it.

Here's why. Set a goal to become millionaire for what it makes of you to achieve it."

Can you say that again please?

"Set a goal to become millionaire for what it makes of you to achieve it."

Multiple Streams of Determination

He said, "Do it for the skills you have to learn and the person you have to become. Do it for what you'll end up knowing about the marketplace, what you'll learn about the management of time and working with people. Do it for the ability of discovering how to keep your ego in check. For what you have to learn about being benevolent. Being kind as well as being strong. What you have to learn about society and business and government and taxes and becoming an accomplished person to reach the status of millionaire.

All that you have learned and all that you've become to reach the status of millionaire is what's valuable. Not the million dollars.

If you do it that way, then once you become a millionaire, you can give all the money away.

Because it's not the money that's really important. What's important is the person you have become."

That was one of the best pieces of philosophy I have ever heard in my life. Nobody ever shared it with me like that before.

Another thing he said was, "beware of what you become in pursuit of what you want. Don't sell out. Don't sell out your principles. Don't compromise your values. Because you might acquire something by doing so, but it won't taste good."

An old prophet said, "Sometimes what tastes good in the mouth finally turns bitter in the belly." Then, later we regret that we compromised or that we did something incredibly wrong to acquire something. It's not worth it. If we do that, then what we get is worthless.

If you use something like that to challenge yourself to grow, to reach a certain level, I think it's wise. Because then you know where the true value is and that is in the person you become.

Defining Moments

I want to reverse back to about 90 seconds ago when you were talking about your great mentor, Earl Nightingale. You talked about the ability to express gratitude. To express thanks.

I feel, in my own life, an aspect of gratitude is very important.

So, number one, do you agree with that, and two, can you talk about the power of that word - gratitude?

Well, it absolutely is very important.

I made a little list the other day as I reminisced about the things that really made such an incredible contribution to my life.

Number one on my list, of course, was my parents.

I was an only child. They spoiled me. They laid a foundation for me that has kept me steady all these years.

The more I thought about it, I thought, 'what a contribution they've made to my life.'

A lot of it, at the moment, I couldn't see. I didn't realize. But, as the years began to unfold, I realized that what they taught me, the care they gave me, the love they shared with me, that no matter what happened to me, I always had a place I could always go home to.

They provided that kind of unique stability.

They didn't just say, 'son, you can do it.' It was also the advice they gave me and the prayers they sent me, no matter where I went around the world, cause I believe in that, the power of prayer.

Every once in awhile I get a letter and someone says, "Mr. Rohn, we are praying for you." I read it and think, 'Wow. This is some kind of letter when someone takes the time to say a prayer."

Multiple Streams of Determination

My gratitude for that is just unending.

Talk about the power of prayer.

Who knows, you know, the mystery of prayer and God.

In the Declaration of Independence it says, we are created equal. But it says also that, we are endowed by our creator with gifts and rights.

It's a philosophy America believes in that we are a special creation. That we have these gifts based on a creator.

We open the Senate with prayer. We put on our money "In God We Trust." We are that kind a nation really.

When I travel the world, people ask me, "how come America does so well?" I say, "read the money." I think that is probably part of it. That kind of trust, that kind of In God We Trust, implies prayer and I think that it is so vital.

It doesn't have to be in a church, synagogue, mosque, or anywhere else. It doesn't have to be in a formal place. But, I think it's a tremendous power.

We're talking about the power of thankfulness, of gratitude.

Jim, I want to put on my world famous, internationally renowned, two-minute warning with you.

All that means is we have about ten minutes left to rock n roll, and shake and bake.

Let's talk about the best-kept secret of the rich, time management. Tell me about the importance of it and how we become effective time managers.

Defining Moments

Well, first is to realize how precious time is.

There's not an unending supply of years in your life.

My father lived to be 93 and it still seemed very short. I kept asking for another ten years, another ten years, another five years.

Surely, Papa can live to be 100, I'd think.

I'd love to have him see the 21 Century, which was not to be. But, ninety-three years still seems short.

The Beatles wrote, "Life is very short." For John Lennon it was extra short. There is not an unending supply of the days and the moments.

The key is to utilize them to the best of your ability. Don't just to let them slip away.

Capture them, like we capture the seasons. There is only so many.

In ninety years you have ninety spring times. If some guy says, you know, "I got twenty more years." You say, "no. You got twenty more times."

If you go fishing once a year you only have twenty more times to go fishing. Now that starts to make it a bit more critical. Not that I have a whole twenty more years, but just twenty more times. How valuable do I want to make these twenty times?

It doesn't matter whether it's going to the concert or sitting down with your family, or taking a vacation. There is only so many.

It's easy not to plan and do the details necessary to make them the best possible.

Then I have other little ideas like, 'don't start the day, until you have it

Multiple Streams of Determination

finished.'

Say that again, Jim.

Don't start the day until you have it finished.

It's a key for executives, a key for leadership. But it's also a key for a mother at home. It doesn't matter, whoever.

Plan the day to the best of your abilities.

There will be plenty of room for surprises and innovations and whatever. Give a good plan, a good schedule for the day.

Because each day is a piece of the mosaic of your life.

You can either just cross your fingers and say, "I hope it will work out okay," or you can give it some attention and say, "here's what I would like to accomplish in the next twenty four hours."

Just look at it that way and do a lot of it up front or maybe the night before. Start the day after you finished it.

It's like building a house. If I asked you, "when should you start building the house that you want to build?" and you say to me, "well, that's a good question. When should I start building the house?" I've got an excellent answer for you. The answer is, you start building it as soon as you have it finished.

You know, someone might say, "is it possible to finish a house before you start it?" The answer is, yes. It would be foolish to start it until you had it finished.

Imagine if you just started laying bricks. Somebody could come by and ask, "What are you building here?" You say, "I have no idea. I'm just laying bricks and well see how it works out." They would call you foolish and maybe take you away to a safe place.

The key is that it's possible to finish a day before you start it. It's possible to finish a month before you start it.

I do business around the world with colleagues in about 50 countries. To do business around the world in 50 countries you can't imagine all of the preparatory planning that has to be done. Some things are three-years, five-years, two-years, one-year ahead in order to do that kind of global business.

But, if you just learned to be disciplined enough to start with the day plan, the month plan, your good health plan, I'm telling you, you will take advantage of time like you can't believe.

Jim, let's bring up a few topics and go 30 to 45 seconds on each, if we can.

You're one of the most effective communicators of the last 50 years or so. You've talked in front of 4 million people and you've influenced millions beyond that through your books and tapes.

What's the most important communication tip you can give us right now?

You just need a desire to be a great communicator and keep improving the art every day. It's easy to be careless with your language in social areas, but that's going to affect your business.

You just have to start practicing the art of better language, whether it's social, personal, home, or family.

You can't say, "oh, it's with my family, so my language doesn't really matter." It really does matter because it's so valuable for them. But, also because it's so valuable for you to practice the art.

Multiple Streams of Determination

It's like this telephone conversation. If I thought, 'well, I don't have 35,000 people to talk to.

So, I'll treat this conversation carelessly.' I just learn not to do that.

I want to give the most concise and best information I can, even though it's a telephone conversation and not a big audience in some auditorium.

So, we're talking here about being on purpose, about changing language, changing your mindset.

When a person goes for something, there are roadblocks to steer away from. There are adversities. Talk about the power of resilience.

You've just got to be able to come back. Come back from a disappointment. It takes a bit of courage.

If you start a sales career and the first person you approach says, "no", you've got to have the courage to talk to the second person.

If you start a little business, set up the first meeting, and nobody joins, you've got to have the courage to say, "I'll set up another meeting. Because if one person says no it doesn't mean everybody's going to say no."

You've just got to have that ability to come back.

You've got to understand the law of averages. Not everybody is going to be interested in your project. Not everybody is going to buy your product.

You can't take it personally.

Then, if you get hit by poor health, you've just got to do everything within your power to get well.

If you face a disappointment, you've got to come back. From a divorce, you've got to come back. It's going to hurt for a while, you've got to let it linger and do whatever it's going to do. But, then you've got to build back.

That's part of the game of life.

It's no different for you, me, or anyone else.

Resilience, we all need it. Whether it's health, marriage, family, business, social, or personal.

Talk about the power of enlightened self-interest.

Yes, life doesn't give us what we need. Life gives us what we deserve.

If you want wealth, it's okay to wish for wealth if you pay the proper price for wealth.

So, there is a price to be paid.

You can pay the proper price without diminishing anyone else. Once I learned that, I got excited about being wealthy in my own self-interest. Everybody wins.

What we're talking about here is coming from a position of integrity and creating wealth for the benefit of others.

I ask this question to a lot of the people, Mark Victor Hansen, Robert Allen, and a lot of the people I have interviewed. I always thought it was a melancholy question, but they have told me it isn't.

We're all going to pass on some day. What do you want the world to say about Jim Rohn when that

day does come?

That he invested his life wisely and as best he could to help as many

Multiple Streams of Determination

people to change their lives as possible and that he blessed his own life. That's really it.

You talk about self-education. You talk about how it's the seed of fortune. Are there any books out there, in addition to your own at jimrohn.com, that you can recommend to my audience?

Well, sure. Shoaff recommended Think and Grow Rich to me when I first started learning.

What was the most powerful thing you took out of Think and Grow Rich?

Desire, determination, preset plans, never give up, persistence, it's got a wealth of information in it.

Anything else come to mind?

The Richest Man in Babylon helped me to become a millionaire by age 32. Simple little book. Easy-to-follow. Inspiring. The Richest Man in Babylon, by George Clauson.

Jim, we're wrapping down the show tonight. Jim, it's been an absolute goldmine and a pleasure to share you with my audience. Jim Rohn, thank you very much for appearing on The Mike Litman Show.

It's been a pleasure, Mike. We'll do it again sometime.